Change Your Mind

Change Your Life

and become one of the Successfuls

Mark Sheppard

Clinical Hypnotherapist

NLP Practitioner

Reiki Master Teacher

First published 2014

ISBN-13: 978-1503164901
ISBN-10: 150316490X

This book is dedicated to Julia whose support and patience went well above and beyond the call of duty during its writing!

Credits and Thanks

There are countless people I could thank for helping me to write this book because during my life they have all played a role in helping to mould the person I have become and in developing the thinking strategies I now use.

With regard to the physical act of writing this book I would particularly like to say a huge thank you to my wife Julia and to my great friend Gwen Steel for the hours they spent proof reading every draft and for their no-nonsense, but always constructive, criticism.

Contents

Change Your Mind
Change Your Life

and become one of the Successfuls

Mark Sheppard

i

Introduction

What is it that makes some people appear happier than others? Why are some people more successful, more powerful or more popular than others? Why is it that some people seem to attract social and professional opportunities while year in, year out, others get completely overlooked? How is it that some people are able to eat whatever they want without gaining weight, while others spend their entire lives dieting and still continue to pile on the pounds? Why do some people love public speaking yet, the very thought of presenting a seminar or delivering a speech, even in front of a few friends, can turn others into jibbering wrecks?

Why do these "Successfuls" always seem to always get the best jobs, know the right people, get paid more for working less, have bigger houses, faster cars, stronger relationships, better health and more friends than the rest of us?

For most of my life I believed that there must be something fundamentally different about these "Successfuls". To me they were the chosen few. I probably thought of them almost as though they were another species; a super-human breed of people. Oh, and yes they even had super human powers, such as the ability to find the last (and usually best) table in a packed restaurant having just walked in off the street. These are the same people who get a seat behind the only short person in a cinema full of basketball players, out on their annual film night. They are the couple who arrive late for a flight only to be up-graded to business class.

You may not know these people personally, but you will most definitely have seen them, heard about them and probably dreamed of being one of them.

I would look at these amazing, powerful, confident, talented, lucky, healthy people and wonder "what special gifts have these chosen few been given that mere mortals like the rest of us have missed out on"? And, like many people I would be very, very jealous – but not just jealous. I would also feel a mixture of anger and guilt.

I was jealous because they clearly had all the things I wanted such as great jobs with gigantic salaries, bucket loads of confidence, oodles of self-esteem and an apparently supernatural influence, not just over other people but over their entire world... and mine too, or so it seemed. Things just appeared to fall into place for the Successfuls, seemingly without them having to make any effort at all. I felt anger because no matter how hard I tried, how much energy I expended, I just could not become one of the Successfuls; there was always some sort of obstacle or some barrier preventing me from living the life I wanted to live, from getting the job I wanted to get and from meeting the people I wanted to get to know. And, let's not forget the "G" word, yes our old friend guilt – after all what would a therapist do if there were no such thing as guilt in the world? I felt guilty for two reasons; first of all having grown up in a deeply religious family, I believed it was wrong to want what others had – after all, "thou shalt not covet thy neighbours ox" – strange because as a young boy growing up in the centre of a city, I cannot for the life of me remember a single neighbour ever owning an ox. There were the usual cats, dogs and rabbits – even the occasional parrot but to the best of my knowledge, no oxen.

Secondly, and probably most demoralising, was the fact that I genuinely felt that I had something to offer. I had ideas, good ideas, and I had a belief in those ideas. I could (when I wanted to) hold a conversation with anyone regardless of their social or educational background. I was practically minded and could turn my hand to most things and yet, for some reason that I could not understand, I just could not become one of the chosen few.

No matter how hard I tried I could not be a Successful. For those of you old enough to remember Boys From The Black Stuff, I was like Yosser Hughes (without the head butting) "*Gizza a job, go on giuz it, go ed*". You see I knew I could be a Successful – I had the skills – but I believed no one would give me the chance to prove it.

No, those damned Successfuls had what I and every other ordinary mortal human being could only dream of having – success, and they had it by the shed load....... or did they?

In 1994 I experienced my first taste of change when it was discovered that I was dyslexic. I'd left school in the late 1970's having just turned 16 years of age and with only a grade 5 GCE in Technical Drawing to my name. I had been considered a remedial student and like many others in the same position as me, I went on to have a succession of low-paid jobs doing unskilled and voluntary work until eventually I found myself working as a volunteer for a charity set up to work with disadvantaged inner-city communities in the wonderful, charming, friendly, multicultural and fun city of Cardiff (yes, I like Cardiff).

I'd somehow ended up on the management committee at Cardiff City Farm and as part of my role I needed to write reports on various projects and issues affecting the day to day running of the site. However, it soon became humiliatingly apparent (at least to me) that something drastic had to be done about my spelling and maths and so I joined an adult education class to study English and arithmetic one day a week. It was while attending these classes that the tutors recognised the signs of dyslexia. This was to have a massive impact on my life and in particular on my beliefs about my own abilities, so much so that in what was probably a rush of blood to the head, I signed up for an Access to Life Sciences course at Llandaff College, Cardiff, and as amazing as it still sounds to me even today, within five years I had gained a Joint Honours Degree in Marine Biology and Zoology and a Masters Degree in Shellfish Biology, Fisheries and Culture – both from the School of Ocean Sciences, UCNW Bangor.

In 2003 I experienced my second taste of change when I underwent hypnotherapy for a phobia. I was 39 at the time and since my early teens I had suffered from an extremely debilitating fear of talking in front of people. I don't mean only public speaking (Glossophobia), though that too, but having to talk to anyone in a formal sense; from a single person to a group of people. Talking socially was fine, I could chat, joke and mess around like anyone else. In fact I even liked (and secretly craved) being the centre of attention - right up to the point some bright spark would say "Mark why don't you tell us about...." or "Mark would you mind introducing yourself". That would be it - instantly I would go into panic mode; my heart would begin to pound uncontrollably in my chest as though it were trying to break its way out of my rib cage; my throat would tighten until it felt as though someone were trying to strangle me; my stomach would start churning like a washing machine; my legs would turn to jelly; my hands would start to shake uncontrollably and my top lip would take on a life of its own and start twitching as though I had suddenly developed some sort of manic tick. I would even get tunnel vision to the point where I was unable to see anything or anyone around me unless they were directly in front of me and even then they seemed so far away, as though I were looking at them through a very long tube. Although I didn't know it at the time, that hypnotherapy session was the first real step in a life-changing process – a journey of self discovery that has allowed me to completely turn my life around.

So, What's This Book All About Then?

Imagine for a moment an ideal world in which you could not fail – what would that world look like? What would you have achieved? And what would you still have left to achieve? What would have to have changed in order for you to have become a "Successful"?

Imagine that after reading this book you wake up one morning and the reality pixies have been working hard all night just for you! You have "the job" and "the social life" that you have always wanted and you also have all of "the things" that you believe you need to in order to make you happy. What would "the job" be? Who would be in "the social life"? Equally importantly who would be out? What would be "the things" that you needed in order to make you happy? When the reality pixies have clocked off and gone home to their loved ones, who is the "successful" you? As one of the Successfuls what do you walk like, talk like, look like? How do you hold your body? What do you sound like? How do you behave and interact with others and with yourself? How do you know you are one of the Successfuls? What is your evidence for success?

What This Book Is Not

This book is not an NLP or hypnotherapy text book. Nor is it an instruction manual on how to live your life. There are plenty of those sorts of book available, some brilliant, some not so brilliant and some that would be better listed under fiction rather than personal development.

If you are looking for someone to tell you who to be, how to behave or how to live your life; if you need someone to tell you how to think and what to believe in, then you need to look for another book because I can't do that. How could I? I may not even know you – we've probably never even met. Now, I'm sure there are plenty of books out there that claim to be able to do all these things – perhaps their authors are psychic! Well unfortunately I'm not, so I don't.

What This Book Is

This book is about how we can all change our lives for the better, how we can discover and ultimately reach our goals and enjoy the successes of our outcomes. This book is also about how we can all take control and responsibility for who we are and what we do and don't do, and how we can create our own reality simply by changing the way that we think and ultimately act.

This book will allow you to discover what "successful" really means to you. It will help you identify the things that stop you from becoming a Successful, to find the resources you already possess and develop the skills needed to build the necessary strategies to become a Successful.

I have written this book to show how, from personal experience, it is not only possible but even easy, to change your life; to take control of your world and become the best that you can be, not just for you but for those around you too. As I've already mentioned, this is not a text book or training manual for life, instead, it's a book based on my own learnings and discoveries born from my experiences of working with hundreds of clients (including and especially myself) from a wide spectrum of social, economic, educational, cultural and religious backgrounds and presenting a wide and diverse variety of issues. And, it's more than that – oh yes... this book comes with value added - it's the story of my own journey and of how I was lucky enough to see the value in the ideas and concepts of personal development, hypnotherapy, NLP and The Law Of Attraction. How I was able to relate those concepts and ideas to my past, incorporate them into my present and use them to change my own life and create a completely new reality; a reality that I wanted and in which I am in control.

At the risk of sounding like the brilliant John Bishop, "I'm just an ordinary bloke from a working class family". This is a semi-autobiographical account of how I, just an ordinary bloke from a working class family, who was told and believed he would never be able to achieve anything and who was only busy watching life pass him by, was able to turn his world on its head. The question is, did I become one of the Successfuls? Well, we shall see....

Part One

What Is It You Want, That You Don't Have Now?

Chapter One

Drawing A Line

Now I know you're probably dying to dive straight in to the deeply profound and totally life-changing concepts and ideas packed like metaphorical sardines into this rather attractive little book - ideas and concepts that will be the fuel in your drive forward along the road to personal development, positive achievement, increased status, becoming a Successful and on, on to world domination.... OK perhaps not world domination but ultimately to discovering what success really means to you, and how you too can become one of the Successfuls.

However, before we can begin working our way towards your goal of becoming one of the chosen few, we need to discover two crucial things which are what it is that you actually want? And where are you now in relation to what it is that you actually want?

Therefore, I think it would be really useful for us to set a benchmark – a starting point if you will as to where you are right now in your life and where the "you right now" is in relation to where you want to get to – your idea of success. It's always good to have a solid reference point that you can look back on in any journey. After all, if you don't know where you started from, how will you know how far you have travelled?

So, let me begin by asking you a question: "What is it you want that you don't have now and what stops you from getting it?"

Exercise 1.

I know, I know - it does seem a little early in the book to be jumping straight into an exercise but please bear with me as it will only take you a few minutes and it's a simple way of creating your starting point. Think of it as a sort of snap-shot of where you are right now on your journey through life in relation to where you ultimately want to be – your goal.

Even if you don't yet know exactly where you want to be or what your idea of successful is, don't worry because you'll still benefit from knowing where you're starting from and, incredible though it may sound, I have genuinely worked with people, who after discovering their starting point, realised they were already where they wanted to be - they were just so busy looking for what they thought they wanted that they had just never taken the time to notice they already had everything they were looking for or working towards!

So let's get started. I wonder if you can imagine that by the time you've finished reading this book something amazing will have happened to the world as you know it. Those wonderful little reality pixies have been busy tweaking away at the laws of causality and now you suddenly find that you have succeeded in everything you did. You reached every goal you ever set for yourself and every single one of your outcomes was positive. Just take a minute or two to close your eyes and imagine what that amazing world looks like. How do you feel in that world? What have you achieved? What, if anything, do you still have left to achieve? Remember this is your ideal world so (sticking to natural, physical and most importantly, legal laws) the only limitation is your own imagination because this is a world where anything is possible.

In Table 1 below, or on a separate piece of paper if you don't want to spoil this lovely book (or it's going on EBay as soon as you've finished with it), in the column under "What Do You Want?" write down the main aspects of your life that you feel are missing, unachievable, out of your reach or not under your control, i.e. the things that you would genuinely like to change, the goals you want to achieve, the things you'd like to accomplish but you feel are out of your grasp for whatever reason.

In the second column headed "What Stops You From Getting It?" write down all barriers and obstacles that are preventing you from reaching or achieving those goals. Make the "What Stops You From Getting It?" list as detailed as possible – who, what, how and why etc. and be as specific as you can, exactly who and what and in exactly what way do they stop you.

Please do not feel you have to try to fill all the rows in Table 1. Just write down as many as you feel you need to – everything you need to make you successful and all the obstacles that you know are preventing you from getting them.

Table 1.

What Do You Want – What Stops You From Getting It?

What Do You Want?	What Stops You Getting It?

NB: Remember to keep in mind natural and physical laws, for example if you happen to be a petite 4'6" tall but you want to be a hulking 6'4", or you've just celebrated your ninety fifth birthday having never done a day's exercise in your life, but you want to be the next Red Bull cliff diving champion then I'm afraid that other than major surgery and/or divine intervention it's just not going to happen.

So, "What is it you want that you don't have now and what stops you from getting it"?

I've been asking my clients this question for quite a few years now and you know what? Almost without fail the reply I hear begins with the words "I don't want.......". Why would that be? When asked what they want why do most clients start their answer with "I don't want ......"?

I wonder if you can picture a scene? Imagine you find yourself waiting tables at a busy restaurant (if you happen to be a waiter or waitress then just imagine that you are at work - sorry). One of the customers catches your eye and you walk over to the table and ask "can I take your order"? To which the diner replies "yes thank you, um.... I don't want the duck because I don't like duck, I don't want the lamb because I just couldn't even think of eating a cute little animal like a lamb, and I definitely do not want the rabbit pie as that's even worse than eating a woolly little lamb...". And so it goes, on, and on and on, with the diner going through the entire menu, telling you every starter, every main course and every dessert that he or she doesn't want to eat and all the reasons that he or she can't or won't eat them.

Now, imagine if this scenario happened with every customer, at every sitting, every single time you try to take an order (I'm sure many people who are actual waiting staff will say that that is exactly what does happen). Imagine if every time you asked them for their orders the diners would tell you all the dishes on the menu that they didn't want to order and give you all the reasons why they didn't want to order them. Apart from thinking there was something wrong with them all, a single sitting could last days. Yet when it comes to considering what it is that we want to achieve, what our goals should be, this is the way most people think, most of the time.

I wonder, if you have a driving licence, did you wake up on the morning of your test and think "Yeah I'm going to get my full licence today" regardless of the fact that you most likely weren't looking forward to the test one little bit and that you were very nervous? Or were your first thoughts "Oh no, I don't want to do my driving test today, I just know I'm going to mess up" or "I don't want to stall the engine or skid the car during an emergency stop" or "I don't want to fail"? The chances are, if your first thought was "yeah I'm going to get my full licence today" or, if you could see yourself throwing away your L-plates then you are very likely to have passed your test first time. For sure you were most likely nervous but your goal was passing your driving test in order to get your full driving licence as opposed to not failing your test and having to remain a learner driver, take more lessons and resit your test.

As we shall see, the difference between thinking of the thing you "do want" as opposed to thinking of the thing you "don't want" is absolutely critical in influencing the eventual outcome of any goal you have.

So, what is it you want that you don't have now and what stops you from getting it?

As a therapist and personal development coach, it makes absolutely no difference whether a client has come to me for therapy, life coaching, sports coaching or business coaching, this is the single most important question I can ask and here's why: By answering the question exactly as it was asked, you are forced to think about the thing or things that you "want" - your goals. It will also bring into focus all the barriers that you "know" are preventing you from reaching them.

Summary

What is it that you "want"? This is a question that should always be answered exactly as it is asked in order that you can begin to focus on your goals. After all if you don't know what you want, how will you know when you get it?

In the next chapter we will look at goals and outcomes and the difference between them. I will also introduce the concept of feedback, both positive and critical.

Chapter Two

Goals vs Outcomes

In the world of personal development there is obviously a great deal of emphasis placed on goals and outcomes. However, unfortunately for some reason the two words are often used interchangeably. Personally I find this incredibly confusing as I believe the two things are mutually exclusive, so for my sake as much as yours, I'd like us to make a clear distinction between "goals" and "outcomes" before we move on.

- A goal is what you want to achieve.

- An outcome is what you actually achieve.

Although they can be, the two things are not necessarily the same. I'm sure we can all remember times when we had a goal but what we ended up with was not at all what we wanted but it was most definitely the outcome we eventually achieved. Remember the old adage "be careful what you wish for".

As a 14 year old boy I was both a fanatical skateboarder and a trainee rock star (I'm still a trainee rock star, although I have pretty much hung up my skateboard – for now). With my friends, I would spend every spare minute (when I wasn't being Jimi Hendrix, Ted Nugent or Tom Petty) trying out new tricks on my skateboard or building ramps and jumps.

One of the skateboarding techniques I really loved doing was something called a catamaran. This involved two or more skateboarders sitting on their boards and linking up side by side using their arms and legs. We would then hurtle down a steep hill locked together as one. What I really liked about doing the catamaran was that the person on the outside would travel incredibly quickly when the catamaran went around a corner – just as a line of ice-skaters do when they turn in a circle, the skater on the inside hardly moves at all while the one on the outside of the line can reach some very exciting speeds.

Every time we would try to go faster than the last time. I particularly remember one occasion when we decided to go down the relatively short but steep hill called Eleanor Close. I was on the outside and we were going for "the all-time world record for me and my mates doing a catamaran down Eleanor Close". We picked up quite a pace as our catamaran careered down the hill and as we approached the right hand bend at the bottom I leaned right back on my board to get as much speed as possible from the centrifugal force as we went into the corner. Just as we were reaching the fastest point my left hand slipped off of my board and my fingers instantly jammed under my left front Day-Glo green Kryptonic wheel (if your heart skipped a beat when I mentioned "catamaran" you were more than likely into skateboarding in the late 70's and you will know exactly what a green Kryptonic wheel is).

My goal was to go faster than anyone else had ever gone around the corner at the bottom of that hill and perhaps I did break "the all time world record for me and my mates doing a catamaran down Eleanor Close" but my outcome, what I actually achieved, was to lose most of the fingernails on my left hand and as a bonus I got a damned good and well deserved telling off from my mum for being such an idiot!

So, your outcome is not necessarily the same as your goal.

- A goal is what you want to achieve.

- An outcome is what you actually achieve.

No Failure, Just Feedback

There is an NLP concept (there are lots of NLP concepts) which goes along the line that "there is no failure, only feedback". It's human nature to want to know how we are doing at any given time and to do this we use feedback in the hope that we will get an objective opinion – even if the feedback is our own. Feedback is something we use in every aspect of our lives, from socialising to relationships to our professional endeavours. In the same way the sensory nerve cells in your hand will let you know when something is hot in order to stop you burning yourself, your psychological feedback system tries to take care of your emotional needs

16

such as self-esteem and confidence and helps you to understand your place in the world.

Just as our nervous system is constantly scanning the world around us and providing biological feedback in order to keep us safe and healthy, our psychological feedback mechanism is doing the same thing to make sure we are fitting in with our social and professional groups, communities, religious beliefs, cultures and so on. Our nervous system provides direct, physical feedback whereas our psychological feedback is much more abstract and based on our core values and beliefs, our perception of the world and our place in it at any given time.

We are all affected by feedback – when it is positive it makes us feel good and boosts our self-esteem. On the other hand, if the feedback comes in the form of a criticism it can have a dramatically negative effect on our self-esteem and our confidence. However, feedback is a critical part of everyone's development and, as with most things, it is only what we believe it to be, based on how we filter it. We will look at how we perceive feedback in more detail later in the book when we talk about The NLP communication model.

"You miss 100% of the shots you don't take".
Wayne Gretzky

With regard to losing my fingernails I definitely didn't get what I wanted to get. That is to say my goal was not the same as my outcome. Instead what I ended up with was a fair bit of pain and a good telling off from my mother. At the time I thought of this as a failure because I didn't do the thing I tried to do but, as with most things we try to do, it is generally ourselves who set the bar and, as we have never done that thing before, we learn as we go along.

So now thinking of it in that context, the feedback I got from that incident was to always wear big thick gloves when skateboarding and, if I was going to do something really stupid and dangerous on a busy main road, not to let my mum find out.

Failure is an inherent part of learning any new skill or attempting something previously untried, but the failure (if there is such a thing) doesn't come from not accomplishing a goal, but from not learning from the experience in order to do it better next time, which will inevitably lead you closer to your goal.

"Those who dare to fail miserably can achieve greatly".
John F Kennedy

Summary

- A goal is what you want to achieve.

- An outcome is what you actually achieve.

- There is no failure only feedback.

- Wear thick gloves when skateboarding.

- Don't let your mum find out.

In the next chapter I will give you a simple but extremely effective method of ensuring that any goal you have will have a positive outcome which I call being on PAR. We will also discuss goals and dreams and why it is important to understand the difference between the two.

Chapter Three

Being on PAR

For any goal to have a positive outcome (i.e. to achieve the result you want), to succeed in anything you put effort in to, there are just three simple yet critical prerequisites you need to satisfy, which I like to think of as being on "PAR"

- A goal must be stated in the Positive.

- A goal must be Achievable.

- A goal must be Realistic.

on PAR

Is Your Goal Positive?

For any goal to have a positive outcome (i.e. to get the thing that you want) it's imperative, for reasons I'll go into later, that your goal is stated in the positive. That is to say that it is something that you feel you want to move towards as opposed to something you want to get away from.

For example, it would be a positive goal to want to move towards a promotion at work so as to have a larger salary, better working conditions and more holidays etc. but it would be a negative goal if all you wanted was to get away from a job you hated doing or a boss you didn't like – or more likely a boss you believe doesn't like you.

Perhaps you're having a disagreement with a friend, partner, colleague or client. In this case it would be a positive goal to look for a peaceful resolution that's a win-win for both parties but a negative goal to try and avoid any potential conflict.

So a positive goal is something that you want to obtain or move towards, whereas a negative goal is something you want to avoid or move away from.

Is Your Goal Achievable?

I have a very good friend called Terry and my mate Terry likes to run marathons. I've no idea why, but apparently there are some people in this crazy old world of ours who find running long distances in all weathers an enjoyable pastime. Terry is one of those people, and he has been running in marathons for many years and without fail, every time I go to watch him take part in a marathon, I become filled with inspiration – I want to be a marathon runner just like my mate Terry. It's even better when he is running in the London Marathon because not only do I love London and jump at any excuse for a visit but also because I can see myself running along the Embankment and into Bridge Street, past Buckingham Palace and along The Mall and on to the final straight – there it is, The Finish Line - I can see it. I can hear the voices of all the spectators crammed along both sides of the road, even the Royal family as they cheer me on from the balcony of the Palace – "come on Mark, come on Mark.... one is almost there – one can do it". And then I cross the finish line.... I've done it...... I've run the London Marathon.

Even writing this has got me thinking about getting my running shoes on and starting my training for the next London

Marathon – but not enough to actually do it, and besides I have a book to write and my publisher has given me a deadline.

However, I can imagine just how utterly amazing it will be, how proud I will feel as I pick up my medal for completing the gruelling 26 mile route. But, is it really physically achievable? Is it actually conceivable that I could one day be physically capable of running in the London marathon? Yes, of course it is. Every year there are more and more ordinary men and women of all shapes, sizes, ages and fitness levels who enter, train for and go on to complete the London marathon and become extraordinary people (or as I see them – Successfuls) and who help to raise millions of pounds for worthy causes.

It also seems that nearly every year there is someone older than the eldest person the year before. In 2008 Buster Martin became the oldest London Marathon entrant at the grand age of 101, although there are those who believe he was only a sprightly 94 years old at the time (like it really makes a difference!). So why haven't I run the London Marathon yet? If Buster Martin can do it and if I get so inspired by my friend

Terry, then why haven't I done it yet? Well if the truth be known I'm not so inspired that I'm prepared to brave the British winters to go for a run on four or five days of the week for hours on end. I did however manage to train for and complete a 10k race at Sherwood Pines in Nottinghamshire a few years ago before deciding to hang up my running shoes because my knees began to complain too much. After a long training run I'd spend the next week walking like John Wayne – It's a good look if you're a cowboy but for a middle-aged therapist it looks more like a case of haemorrhoids than horse rustling!

Is Your goal Realistic?

We all have dreams and aspirations. I'm a bit of a science geek which is why I chose to study for a science degree rather than an arts degree. I have always been fascinated by the idea of space travel and in an ideal world where anything was possible it would be my goal to travel to another planet such as Mars or Europa, one of Jupiter's moons. I would love to be amongst the first human beings to set up a new colony, to be at the forefront of space exploration and discovery. As Captain Kirk might say "to explore strange new worlds, to seek out new life forms and civilization, to boldly go where no man has gone before....." (sorry I got a bit carried away!). But is travelling to another planet really an achievable goal for me? I don't mean the whole Star-Trekky thing of seeking out new life forms and the like, just the going to Mars: is it realistic?

I'm sure that for someone, some day it will be but for me it's not an achievable goal for several reasons. Firstly I'm not an astronaut - my degrees were in marine biology and zoology and neither Mars nor Europa are known for their abundance of marine life, at least not yet. Nor am I ever likely to be an astronaut. Secondly, a manned trip to Mars, Europa or any other planet that isn't our own moon is probably not going to happen in my lifetime, or at least not until I'm a very old man, by which time NASA is unlikely to want me – not unless they want to set up the first Martian retirement home. Thirdly and without doubt most importantly, my wife would never allow it!

It's one thing to have a goal but it's another to put all of your time and energy into something that will never, ever, happen no matter how badly you want it and how hard you try or how many times you wish for it, simply because it is not on PAR. Buster Martin's goal was to take part in the London Marathon.

His goal was not to win it; that would have been completely unrealistic for the obvious reason that at 101 years of age, or even at a sprightly 94, his body was simply not able to perform at the necessary level to compete with the world's elite runners like Emmanuel Mutai who in 2011 completed the London Marathon in an amazing time of 2:04:39. Had Buster's goal been to win the London marathon he would soon have become demoralised and lost all of his motivation. He would most certainly have over trained and caused himself a serious injury which would have put him out of the marathon altogether. Instead, Buster's goal was to enter and take part in the race and it answered all three prerequisites; it was Positive, Achievable and Realistic. So, is your goal on PAR?

- - - - **P**ositive **A**chievable **R**ealistic - - - -

Exercise 2.

Now take another look at the answers you gave to Exercise 1. In Table 1 under the "What Do You Want?" column how many of your answers are on PAR? For now, don't worry about the answers you have given in the second column, what is important at this point is that you are objectively critical as to whether or not your goals are stated in the Positive, they are physically Achievable and they are Realistic. So again, and be totally honest with yourself, how many answers are actually positive goals? That is to say that you want to move towards something as opposed to you wanting to move away from, or avoid something? How many of your answers are physically achievable for you – even if it requires years of training? And how many are realistic – will it happen in your life-time, do you have, or can you gain the skills and/or physical ability needed however long it takes etc.?

If you find that any of your answers are not on PAR then now is the time to either let them go or to make some adjustments to them to bring them on PAR. Or, simply accept them for what they are: dreams.

There is nothing wrong with having amazing goals but as I mentioned earlier, if you are putting all your time and energy into something that will either never realistically happen or is not under your control then you will inevitably become demoralised and demotivated and sooner or later you will give up and believe you have failed and your self-esteem will inevitably suffer.

Summary

- A goal is something you want to achieve.

- A positive goal is something that you want to move towards or achieve.

- A negative goal is something you want to avoid or move away from.

- An outcome is what you actually achieve regardless of your goal.

- For any goal to be successful it must:

- be stated in the Positive.

- be Achievable.

- be Realistic.

- - - - **P**ositive **A**chievable **R**ealistic - - - -

on PAR

Chapter Four

Dreams vs Goals

Perhaps now would be a good time to make a distinction between what constitutes a dream and what constitutes a goal.

Unless you are a devout Buddhist who has already found enlightenment, the chances are that you will have at least one dream. We all (excluding the enlightened) have dreams; things we would love to do or achieve in a perfect world where absolutely anything is possible – as I've said, one of my dreams is to travel to another planet and who knows, one day NASA may be looking for a middle aged therapist with a degree in marine biology, who occasionally walks like John Wayne and they'll give me a call – but I won't hold my breath for that day to arrive.

We often hear of people fulfilling their dreams or talking about a dream come true, such as young girl out shopping with her mother when she is spotted by a modelling agent and whisked off to become the next super model. Then of course there are the lucky lottery winners whose lives are changed overnight.

A dream is something that may or may not be possible – something we would like to happen. Yes it's absolutely true to say that dreams do come true, for some people – I don't want you to think I'm a total killjoy! But just like winning a raffle or being struck by lightning, the outcome is not under our control. You could spend all your time working to earn money for lottery tickets only to die of old age without ever winning a penny. In the same way you could win the Euro roll-over with the first and only ticket you ever buy. Wow! It would be fantastic, amazing and for most people a real dream come true (would it make you a Successful?) but it was never under your control.

A goal on the other hand is something that is achievable however difficult it is to reach or however long it might take to achieve. Yes goals can be dreams at the same time but dreams can only be goals if they are on PAR. A dream is something we want or would like to happen but is either not on PAR or not under our control for whatever reason. A goal on the other hand is something that we are willing to work for and is completely on PAR.

Travelling through space to be part of the first colony on another planet is a dream I've had since childhood but it's a dream, because it's not under my control – it may happen just as one day I may win the lottery, NASA may call me, but it's not my choice, not under my control and therefore not on PAR – it's my dream. As I've said, we all have dreams, it's good to have dreams and sometimes they do come true – but it's not a good idea to watch your life pass you by while waiting for one to come true.

Summary

- A dream is a goal that is not under your control.

- Dreams can come true but it is not by your doing.

- It's good to have dreams.

- We all have dreams (except the enlightened).

In the next chapter I will talk about the importance of motivation in achieving our goals and the affect that negative or positive motivation will have on determining the outcome of any goal.

Chapter Five

Motivation

Whenever we do something, anything, anything at all, whatever action we take to accomplish a goal, whether it be running a Marathon, breaking the four minute mile, climbing a mountain, presenting a seminar, losing weight, stopping smoking, starting smoking, committing a crime, solving a crime, learning to play an instrument, making love, putting the kettle on or simply changing channels on the TV - even writing a personal development book, whenever we do anything there has to be something that motivates us to do it.

Motivation is like gravity; an invisible, untouchable force attracting something (you) to a given point (your goal). Once we are motivated to act (when we are in motion) the effort we put in to achieving our goal is dependant on a law similar to

Newton's First Law of Motion "every object in a state of uniform motion tends to remain in that state of motion unless an external force is applied to it". Basically, if we are not motivated we are "at rest" and will remain at rest for ever unless we are acted on by an external force i.e. hunger, fear, pain, desire (motivation). Once in motion (motivated) an object will only come to rest when it meets an equal and opposite force (our goal). Just like the book in your hand or your bottom on the chair (assuming you're sitting on a chair of course) they are not falling because the force acting on them (gravity) is matched by an equal and opposite force (your hand and the chair). Motivation differs from gravity however in that it stops as soon as a goal is achieved whereas gravity never, ever stops.

If you need to complete a task or reach a goal then your motivation must be equal to, or greater than the effort needed to complete that task. For example, if you are a bit peckish but it hasn't been too long since you last ate then you are not likely to be highly motivated to get some food. However, if you have been doing hard physical work for many hours with nothing to eat, then your motivation is likely to be high enough for you to put a lot of effort into getting food.

Mark's Universal Laws of Motivation

- Motivation is the driving force behind every goal.

- A person will only act when motivated to do so.

- In order to complete any task the motivational force needed must be equal to, or greater than any opposing force.

- Negative motivation will cause a person to move away from something.

- Positive motivation will cause a person to move towards something.

- Motivation stops when a goal is achieved.

Can you remember a time when you were really motivated? Perhaps it was to win a race or to get away from a vicious dog. Maybe saving for your first car or your first house. Perhaps it was when you were trying to impress a new love in your life, or later, planning a wedding. How much energy did you have then? How much did you get done? What did you accomplish? Now, compare those occasions with the times when you weren't at all motivated – when there was nothing happening in your life that inspired you - a time in your life when you were bored. How much did you get done then? What, if anything, did you accomplish?

Motivation is the driving force behind anything that anyone has ever done, from getting out of bed in the morning to building a skyscraper to going to the moon. If there was no motivation we wouldn't do anything to change the situation we are in at any given time; why would we? A life without any form of motivation would be the equivalent of an object being placed in space – free from gravity. It would remain there motionless until the end of its days unless acted upon by some external force.

What is your motivation for reading this book? I'll ask you again at the end of this chapter! And again at the end of the book!

Positive and Negative Motivation

When we choose to do something, anything at all, there are two types of motivational force that can compel us to act; positive and negative. Although complete opposites, both are equally powerful and can instil in us enough drive to help us accomplish even the biggest of tasks. However, no matter what our goal, whether or not the outcome that we eventually achieve is a positive one or a negative one will always depend on whether or not the motivational force was positive or negative. There are many things that can motivate us to act such as love, compassion, fear, hate, distrust, lust, greed, hunger or thirst to name but a few. When was the last time you felt really motivated to do something? What was it that last motivated you? What was the outcome you actually achieved–negative or positive?

NB: I deliberately left "money" out of the above list of things that can motivate us. Although many people believe they and/or others are motivated by money this is not actually the case. Money can be one of two things depending on the use of the word – it is inanimate objects such as coins and bank notes etc., but it's also a concept. Money in and of itself cannot "do" anything "to" us. It certainly could not be the source of all evil. However, a love of money, a greed for money or a desire for the power money can bring, or the material things it can give us, even a hatred of money are all extremely powerful motivating forces.

Negative Motivation

When we act out of negative motivation we are trying to move away from, or avoid something. For example, many people will do almost anything to avoid conflict, maybe with a boss over working hours or pay, perhaps with a partner over housework, or even, who's going to drink while the other drives on a night out.

Have you ever wanted to tell a friend something about them that maybe you find annoying or embarrassing but in the end you didn't because you were worried that you may offend, upset or hurt them, and maybe even lose their friendship? That is a classic example of negative motivation – you are moving away from or avoiding conflict or the possibility of hurting your friend or losing their friendship.

Emily and Jane were both in their late 20's / early 30's, were best friends and had been since primary school. They had grown up together, fallen in love with the same pop stars and even fallen in love with the same men and then fallen out with each other over falling in love with the same men. They had gone on holidays together, lived together when they left home and they would often go out on the town together. Both women took the greatest of care in their appearance and always made an effort to look their absolute best whatever they were doing.

As often happens as we get older Jane had been gradually putting on weight, particularly around her tummy but despite this she still wore the same type and size of clothes she had always worn on nights out. Now, Emily could see that Jane's clothes were no longer fitting her properly around the middle, but despite this, she kept quiet because she did not want to say anything that may have hurt her best friend's feelings. On one particularly warm summer's Saturday night they had decided to go a to a certain bar together because Jane knew there was a good chance that a man who had recently started work for the same company she worked for was likely to be there and Jane really wanted a chance to meet him socially.

So after a not inconsiderable amount of time doing her hair and make-up and choosing the perfect outfit, then a different perfect outfit and another perfect outfit before deciding on the original perfect outfit, Jane met up with Emily for their night out and a possible romantic encounter. However, as soon as Emily spotted Jane and saw what she was wearing she knew her friend would be devastated if she realised just how badly fitting her clothes were and exactly how big they made her look, especially around the tummy. But, again, rather than telling her how she really looked, she did the complete opposite and told Jane she looked lovely, which of course boosted Jane's self-esteem and made her even more excited about the possible romantic evening ahead.

So, as the girls jump excitedly into a taxi for the short drive in to town, let us jump forward a few hours and sure enough we find Emily and Jane in the same bar as the work colleague Jane wants to get to know. Eventually, full of self-esteem, confidence and several glasses of wine, Jane picks up the courage to walk over and say hello to her Mr Right. She was both pleased and relieved as he seemed genuinely glad to see her and they begin having quite a cosy little chat – all well and good. It was at some point during that quite cosy little chat that Mr Right asked Jane when her baby was due!! OMG!!

When I met Jane, her confidence was shattered, she was suffering from depression, had no social life, she'd left her job and she had not spoken to Emily since that fateful night more than two years earlier. You see, Emily's "intended" outcome was positive, it was for Jane to be happy but, because her goal was "not" to upset or hurt her best friend by telling her how she really looked, her motivation was negative. The word "not" tells us that the motivation was negative and that Emily, despite her best intentions was moving away from or avoiding something, in this case conflict with, or hurting, her best friend's feelings. Her goal was positive but negatively motivated which could only ever end with a negative outcome.

As I've mentioned, negative motivation is a very powerful force – just as powerful as positive motivation.

The diet industry (a multi-billion pound concern) is powered entirely by negative motivation because it feeds (pardon the pun) on your vulnerabilities, on your fears, low self-esteem and negative self-image. Nobody ever starts a diet when they are feeling empowered, when their self-esteem and confidence is at its highest. No one looks in the mirror and thinks "yeah... I look really good, I feel really good, I think I'll go on a diet".

By their very nature diets force the dieter to focus on getting away from all the things they don't want such as unsightly fat or cellulite, feeling as though their health is being affected and having low self-esteem because they believe they look unattractive.

The very act of being on a diet forces you to think about all the food you can't eat while you're on your diet so that you spend all of your time trying to avoid food and therefore, ironically focusing on it. As we shall see a little later you cannot not think of something.

When I ask clients why they want to lose weight there are several answers that I usually get:

- "I don't want to be fat any more".
- "I don't want to have health problems in the future".
- "I hate the way I look".
- "My clothes don't fit me".
- "I used to love going out but now I don't because people look at me and think I'm greedy".

(Remember waiting on tables in chapter one - all the things we don't want?).

At first glance these may sound like good reasons to want to lose weight and to some extent i.e. logically, they are. However it's not the "intended" outcome that's the problem here but the motivation behind it. Each of the above answers are driven by negative motivation and as we will see, thinking strategies powered by negative motivation are always going to throw up a whole heap of problems.

This is crucial in understanding why, in the long-term, for most people, diets do not work.

I get similar answers from clients who want to stop smoking. When I ask them for their reason for wanting to stop they will say things like:

- "I don't want to die of lung cancer".
- "I don't want to die young".
- "It costs too much money".
- "It's anti-social".
- "I don't want my kids to copy me".

Negative motivation will almost always produce a negative outcome because it will cause you to want to move away from, or avoid something. The problem then is that we will have to focus on the thing we want to avoid, which will always create two immovable barriers; firstly is The Law Of Attraction which I will talk about a little later in the book, and, secondly, when we focus on the thing we are trying to get away from, we don't have a clear, positive goal. It's a bit like escaping a desert island in a boat that has no rudder, with no idea of which direction to take – "I hate this island", "I must get off this island", "ha ha I'm off that island at last". OK, you're off the island but now what? You have no destination; you're completely at the mercy of the wind, tides and currents – you are under the control of the elements and the environment in which you now find yourself.

When I was a young boy I lived in Plymouth with my family and during the summer holidays we'd often drive up on to Dartmoor if the weather was good – anyone who knows Dartmoor well will tell you that unless you're a masochist, lost, or training to be a Marine Commando, when the weather is good is the only time to drive up on to Dartmoor!

To me, Dartmoor is one of the jewels of the British countryside, with sweeping hills, lush valleys, beautiful rivers and meandering streams, rocky outcrops, chocolate-box villages and wild Dartmoor ponies wandering freely over the moor. Like many beautiful but untamed places Dartmoor can also be one of the most inhospitable and dangerous environments to visit, especially in winter. The weather can change in an instant on the moors, even in summer, because it's high up and so is very exposed to the elements. There are treacherous marshes and thick fogs, which we used to call "pea-soupers", which can descend in minutes and last from a few hours to several days.

However, in the summer when the weather is good it really is a magical and inspiring place and I have lots of wonderful childhood memories of climbing rocks, fishing with nets for sticklebacks in the streams and swimming in the rivers. At the time my father worked for The Goodyear Tyre & Rubber Company and he'd always manage to get hold of a huge tractor-tyre inner tube which he'd blow up before we left the house. I can still see him clearly tying the massive inflated inner-tube to the roof of our car – I'd hate to think how much extra fuel he used due to wind resistance as we drove for an hour or more from Plymouth up on to the moors (of course in the late 60's fuel was considerably cheaper than it is today but

I suppose everything is relative given that salaries were much lower too). Along with my brothers and sister I'd spend hours playing in the river with our ginormous inner-tube.

My mother would always put together a wonderful picnic of far too much food, that me and my afore mentioned siblings would still manage to fight over. As a bonus if we were very well behaved we'd usually find an ice-cream van on the way home or if we were really lucky (and very, very well behaved), we'd stop for a proper Devonshire cream tea of home-made scones, strawberry jam and of course proper Devonshire clotted cream. However, despite the amazing scenery and all the fun (and clotted cream) we enjoyed, as a young boy, the one thing that fascinated me most about Dartmoor was the infamous Dartmoor prison. I can always remember looking out of the window of the car hoping to get a glimpse of that notorious, mythical – and for a 6 year old boy, totally scary place. What fascinated me most wasn't the prison itself but the stories of all the poor souls who had tried to escape. I always semi hoped (and feared) that I'd see an escaped convict. We did use to pass working parties of prisoners as we drove along (if my memory serves me right) but it was the idea of seeing the fleeting glimpse of a dark figure ducking behind some rocks or running across a field that I always hoped, and simultaneously feared to see.

There is a very good reason why Dartmoor prison is where it is. Other than the two roads that run close to it, the prison is surrounded on all sides by miles of barren rocky hills and dangerous bogs, so any prisoner who manages to get out of the confines of prison itself will still have to escape the moor and therefore the environment in which they find themselves. Here the escapee has only two options; firstly they could take to the roads – not likely as they will be easily spotted and quickly picked up and secondly, they could go over the moor.

As you can imagine, a place like Dartmoor Prison produces many stories including tales of escaped convicts getting lost on the moor only to be picked up sometime later, cold, hungry and exhausted, or worse. It was said that some would walk in circles for days only to end up right back at the prison. There were even tales of prisoners becoming so hungry and exhausted after days of walking around and around in circles that they would give themselves up or make their way back to the prison, knock on the door and ask to be let back in.

Like you I'm sure that many of these tales have been, let's say, embellished a little over the years but they are perfect metaphors for negative motivation. The escaped prisoners weren't trying to get anywhere in particular, they were simply trying to get anywhere that wasn't Dartmoor Prison. "I hate this prison", "I must get out of this prison", "ha ha I'm out of that prison at last". OK, you're out of the prison, but now what? Once they were outside of the prison walls they had left their metaphorical desert island and were now direction-less and drifting in their equally metaphorical rudderless boat, completely at the mercy of the elements and the environment in which they had found themselves, literally.

I'm sure there were some escapees that had a fixed destination in mind and a plan on how to get there when they left the prison and I would hazard a guess that they were the ones that manage to get the furthest before being picked up.

In Table 2 we can see how negative motivation can produce a negative outcome even if a goal is positive.

Table 2.

Goals - Negative Motivation - Outcomes

Goal	Negative Motivation	Outcome
To get another job	To get away from boss	Had to start from bottom in new company – new boss worse than last one
To lose weight	Stop being fat and unhealthy	Lost weight at first using willpower but put it all and more back on because of constantly thinking about food. Health affected

When we are negatively motivated to act, we will always, most definitely, without any shadow of a doubt end up somewhere! But where we end up, who knows, because our destination will never be controlled by us but by the environment and the elements in which we find ourselves.

Positive Motivation

To be driven by positive motivation is to move towards something, it's your positive goal, it's where you're going, it's moving towards the thing you want. As Sue Knight says in her excellent book NLP At Work "People who achieve what they want in life have compelling goals" and who on Earth would be compelled to move towards the thing they are trying to avoid. Living to a ripe old age, passing your driving test, enjoying life, being in a loving relationship are all compelling because they are goals driven by positive motivation.

Take a look at Table 3 and compare these two sets of goals. How do each of these sets of goals makes you feel?

Table 3.

Positively vs Negatively Motivated Goals

Positive Goal	Negative Goal
Becoming fitter, slimmer and healthier because I want to set a good example for my children, have a better quality of life and live longer.	Not wanting to be unfit, fat and ill because I don't want to set a bad example for my children, have a poor quality life and die young.

How do you feel when you think of not being fat, of not being unfit, not being ill and not dying young of an obesity related condition? Now compare that with how you feel when thinking of being fitter and healthier and living a long, happy and successful life. Which of these two sets of goals do you want to move towards?

Logically these two sets of goals should mean the same thing, i.e. not being ill should mean the same as being healthy. However, at an unconscious level they mean completely opposite things. The negatively motivated goals (prefixed by "not" in the above examples) force you to focus on the things you don't want – on the very things you are trying to get away from but never on where you want you go or what you want to achieve. The positive goals however show your unconscious mind exactly what you want to achieve which in the above scenario is you looking fitter, slimmer and healthier, setting a good example for the children and living to a ripe old age. By having a positive goal you give your unconscious mind pictures of what you actually want, which as we will see, is so important in allowing you to reach a positive outcome.

What do you think of when you think of being on holiday? For many people it's relaxing by a pool or on a beach, warm sunshine, good food and enjoying the company of friends and family. For others it could be adventure, visiting exotic new places and meeting new people. However, whether you want a relaxing holiday or adventure and excitement, the thought of it is so compelling that you want to move towards it no matter how much effort it takes. Look at the work most of us have to put in for us to achieve our perfect holiday. We can spend hours and hours looking though brochures or searching the internet, just to find the package that's right for us. We may have to buy new clothes or specialist equipment, we have to choose what to take, pack everything we may need, travel to the airport, spend hours on an aeroplane, put up with jet lag, then do most of it again on the way home, and yet somehow, we still enjoy our holidays. Added to that lot is that fact that it usually costs a small fortune for the privilege. How many things that you do not want to do would you really put that much effort into?

If you know you are good at your job and you believe you're worth much more than you're currently being paid, if you want to earn more money so you can give yourself and your family a better standard of living, then looking for a better employer who'll offer you a higher salary, fewer hours and better working conditions is obviously positively motivated. When we are positively motivated we focus on the things we want and we naturally begin to move towards them.

To use the desert island analogy again, if you want to get to the mainland you would first have to decide where you think it is and this will give you a direction in which to sail. You would then have to build the most suitable raft or boat possible given your limited resources and devise some way of steering, such as a rudder in order for you to navigate towards your goal. You would also have to include some form of power source like a sail or a paddle in order to get you there more quickly. If you thought the journey was going to take some considerable time you may also want to build some form of shelter to protect you from the elements and you'll need to stock up with as much food and water as possible. Thinking of what you "want" or where you "want" to go will allow you to work out what resources you will need and what you will have to do in order for you to reach your goal. You will then be in control of your direction and have the means to get there. You will have control, or at least a great deal more control, over the environment in which you chose to place yourself than you would if you had simply wanted to just get off the island. Even if the weather turned nasty and the sea became rough you would still have a much better chance of getting to where you wanted to go than if your goal had been simply to get off the island. If your only concern is to get off the island then the only resource you will need is something that floats such as a boat, a raft or even just a log and off you go, but where you ended up and when you got there would be totally out of your control.

So, what was your motivation for reading this book? Was it positive or negative? Were you trying to get away from something such as low self-esteem, a fear of giving presentations, not wanting to fail in your career, not wanting to be unpopular with your peers or feeling as though you were not in control of your life? Or, were you trying to move towards something such as moving up the social or career ladder, increasing your self-confidence, improving your personal and/or professional relationships? Were you fed up of being unsuccessful or were you trying to become one of the Successfuls? Has your motivation changed?

Whether you were negatively or positively motivated to read this book makes no difference up to this point. The important thing is to understand the difference between negative and positive motivation and to see that by simply changing or re-framing your goals so that you are positively motivated, you will have a much greater chance of achieving a positive outcome.

Summary

Mark's Universal Laws of Motivation

1. Motivation is the driving force behind everything we do.
2. A person will only act when motivated to do so.
3. In order to complete any task the motivational force needed must be equal to or greater than any opposing force.
4. Negative motivation will cause a person to move away from or avoid something.
5. Positive motivation will cause a person to move towards a thing.
6. Motivation stops when a goal achieved.

We all possess within us all the resources needed to achieve any goal so long as that goal is on PAR. By re-framing our goals so that they become compelling we become positively motivated.

In part two we will look at all the things that we believe are stopping us from getting exactly what we want. We will also look at the reasons why we don't always get what we want or achieve the things we know we are capable of achieving.

Part Two

What Stops You From Getting It?

Chapter six

It, They, Them, That

OK, so by now you should hopefully know what it is that you want and whether it's a dream or a goal, whether or not it is on PAR and whether or not you are positively or negatively motivated. Hopefully you are now positively motivated because all of your goals are things you want to move towards (if you're not it may be a good idea to re-read part one and to have another go at the exercises). So now it's time to look at what stops you from getting it.

Throughout your life, how many of your goals have been put on hold or have never even gotten off the ground because of some outside influence? At some time or other, most of us will have heard someone say something like "oh I would have loved to do….." or "when I was younger I always wanted to …......". I guarantee that if I were to ask them why they had not achieved their goals, most if not all would say things that would tell me it was because they were either not on PAR or they had given responsibility for achieving their goal to my good friends "It, They, Them, That".

Maybe you have struggled to reach goals that you know you should have been able to reach – things you were more than capable of achieving. Maybe you didn't get that promotion you knew you deserved because your boss didn't like you, or couldn't see your full potential and instead it was given to one of the Successfuls. Perhaps you've always struggled with personal relationships because your partners never listened to you, or never really understood you?

"I could have been a footballer, but I had a paper round".
Yosser Hughes.

How many goals do you still have? How many of those have you made any headway towards achieving? How many projects, ideas, ambitions and jobs are just sitting there on the back burner while you wait for "the right moment"?

Let's go back to your answers in Table 1 and look again at the reasons, barriers and obstacles that you "know" are stopping you from achieving your goals.

As I've mentioned earlier in the book, for most of my life I suffered from a debilitating phobia of speaking formally in front of people; any people, groups or individuals. It didn't seem to matter if I was put on the spot or if I had time to prepare, the outcome was always the same - before I got to open my mouth to speak I would fly into full-on panic mode. In fact it was probably worse if I did have time to prepare because it meant I would be in a growing state of fear for longer and the longer I had, the more terrifying it would become. I would start to think about "it" months beforehand. As the fateful day loomed ever closer I would become more and more stressed until all I could think of was "the talk". I wouldn't be able to sleep, I would become ill, and I wouldn't be able to concentrate or focus on anything except the talk - eventually not even on the event itself.

Now, I'm not talking only about giving a formal talk such as a presentation or a speech but any situation in which I knew (or even suspected) I would have to speak, such as a job interview or attending a training event, where, inevitably, some bright spark would ask everyone to introduce themselves "as a bit of an ice-breaker" - why do people do that? Even now I still don't understand the reason behind it and it's something I wouldn't do during a seminars or training event.

In fact, any situation in which there was the slightest possibility that I would be asked to say something or give an opinion would turn me into a jibbering wreck.

"I usually end up jibbering absolute talkish".
Hugo Horton.

By the day of the talk "it" had grown in to a demon, a monster ready to devour me, to make me look like a total and utter knob-head in front of my peers. "It" was a monster created for one purpose – to prove to the world that I was an incompetent, jibbering fool who would never be able to speak in front of people without falling to pieces. I knew "it" would make me appear like someone who should never get "that" job, someone who could not be trusted with the simplest of tasks.

Anyone lucky enough to have never suffered from a phobia of public speaking – or any other phobia for that matter - will think that this all sounds overly dramatic, but for those affected, it's very real, extremely debilitating and absobloodylutely terrifying – I kid you not!

So, what does this have to do with "What Stops You From Getting It"?

If the truth be known I have always been a bit of a closet performer (yes I do realise that could be taken in more ways than one – that's your issue not mine). For as long as I can remember I've admired amazing entertainers, actors, politicians and great orators; people who have the ability to captivate an audience and have them mesmerized or crying with laughter or sadness almost instantly. As a child I would watch, spellbound as people (such as the now Sir Bruce Forsyth) would have the audience eating out of their hands within seconds of walking on to the stage. I so wanted to be able to do what they could do – to captivate an audience, to show the world I did know what I was talking about, that I was capable and competent – that I wasn't a total and utter knob-head.

I was in absolute awe of their relaxed confidence, their sense of self-worth and self-belief in their abilities as public speakers, whilst I would fall apart at the merest hint of having to talk in front of people. Even now as an adult, with all my years of accumulated knowledge and life experiences and all the training and the experience I've gained as a therapist, I am still just as in-awe of these entertainers as I was when I was a child.

A little while back, I was lucky enough to see one of my comedy heroes, the hilariously brilliant Rhod Gilbert, performing his "The Man with the Flaming Battenberg Tattoo" show at the Royal Concert Hall in Nottingham. As I took my seat and looked at the stage on which there was just a small table and a stool, my excitement was palpable, not just because I knew I was going to be laughing for the next two hours or so but also because I knew I was going to watch a great performer walk onto a virtually empty stage and captivate an entire audience, within seconds. And, I have to say, I was not disappointed. Not only does he live in the wonderful, friendly and welcoming city of Cardiff (I told you I had a soft spot for the city), Mr Gilbert is also a comedy genius. Like other excellent entertainers, Rhod Gilbert was able to captivate, enthral, interact with and lead the entire audience at the pace that he set.

So, what was stopping me from being like them? Like Rhod Gilbert or Sir Bruce? I don't mean what was stopping me from having their phenomenal talent (that's a whole different ball game – or a book perhaps!) but their confidence and self-belief. "It, They, Them That" was stopping me from being like them, just as "It, They, Them, That" stops everyone who has ever been prevented from reaching every single goal in their lives that was on PAR.

So who or what is or are "It, They, Them, That"?

It, They, Them, That is everything and everybody you believe stops you from reaching your goal. In my case, as far as public speaking is concerned, It, They, Them, That went right back to my school days.

Children are little learning machines. It's programmed into every cell in their bodies. From the moment we are born, in fact even before that; while we were still in the womb, our brains work like learning sponges soaking up every bit of information they come across.

My time at primary school holds lots of great memories for me. I liked my school and my teachers and I made some really good friends. I went to a lovely school in Barry, South Wales and if my memory serves me well I believe the headmaster at the time was a wonderful man by the name of Mr Gill. Although Mr Gill could be quite strict (and a bit scary to a 7 – 11 year old) he had a way of making his pupils feel confident, as though they had something to offer.

Yes Holton Road Junior School was a great little school full of happy little learning machines. In fact, if you promise not to tell anyone I'll let you in to a 40ish year old secret - even though I was still only in junior school this was the very first time I ever fell in love – no not with Mr Gill! It was with a girl in my class. She was the most beautiful girl I had ever seen! She was very, very, very clever - she knew all the answers to all the questions, whatever the subject. She even knew how to make ginger beer – how cool is that? She could sing and play the guitar and she could remember all the words to Puff The Magic Dragon. She was of course my teacher, though to my shame I cannot remember her name. It was because of her that I did what I believe to be my first really courageous act.

All the schools in the area were invited to put on a show at the Barry Memorial Hall – a very large venue by the way! Our school was staging a production of Peter and the Wolf but, with only days to go before the big night, the boy playing the duck emigrated to Australia with his family. Now, Miss Whom To My Shame I Cannot Remember Her Name, was quite upset by this act of betrayal and desertion as it was her production and she was very proud of the work everyone had put in so far. So, one morning during assembly she asked if anyone would step in and play the part of the duck – a fairly substantial role I should add! Obviously I could not bear to see the love of my life so distraught and so, even though I was a shy little boy who used to blush when his name was called during the taking of the register, I put my hand up and volunteered. I felt like a hero, like Peter himself who had just rescued the beautiful Princess Miss Whom To My Shame I Cannot Remember Her Name from the clutches of an evil wolf. Even better was to come though because on the big night, after the show had finished, Princess Miss Whom To My Shame I Cannot Remember Her Name came in to the

dressing room and actually gave me a kiss on the cheek! .....
A kiss! On the cheek!

However, if my primary school memories are of fun, laughter and love, my secondary school memories are the complete opposite.

From the moment I moved up to Barry Boys Comprehensive School I seemed to spend most of my time in a state of terror. I was terrified of the school, terrified of the teachers, terrified of the headmasters, terrified of the numbers of students in the school. I also started to struggle with a lot of my school work – something which had never shown itself at primary level and which I now put down to the different methods of teaching. At primary school, lessons were very hands-on and interactive, whereas the mode of teaching at my secondary school was much more talk and chalk and ducking blackboard erasers thrown by psychopathic teachers (obviously these are my subjective memories – I'm sure other memories are available).

Although I was genuinely interested in almost all of the subjects I was taught at school (I have always loved learning and still do), I continually struggled to achieve. My marks were consistently poor and my school reports were the same year in year out - "could do better", "needs to concentrate more during lessons", "must try harder", "is capable of much better work" (I'm sure these are all statements that will sound familiar to many people reading this book). I would dread taking my end of year reports home to my parents for several reasons, not least of which was that I wanted them to be proud of me, but every year I felt that I had let them down. I thought they believed I wasn't trying hard enough and I really did want to get good marks and I genuinely worked hard for them. Yet however hard I tried, I never achieved the marks I knew I was capable of getting and could not for the life of me understand why.

Something that became very apparent at secondary school was that I had a real problem reading out-loud. For some reason, the words I said out-loud were not always the words that were written on the page and yet when I read to myself I didn't seem to have this problem. Nowadays this would hopefully be picked up very early on in a child's development, but it wasn't until I was in my 30's that it was discovered I was dyslexic.

Dyslexia can affect different people in many different ways and for me, three of the ways in which I'm affected are firstly that the words tend to move around the page of their own free will; secondly I often see different words to those that are actually on the page and thirdly I have never mastered the art of forward reading. This is fine if I'm reading to myself because by the time I have reached the end of a sentence I can sort out the misread words in my head according to the context of whatever I'm reading. For example I might read "the man talked into his horse and went straight to the chicken" which is obviously not a logical statement but in the context of a story it might actually read "the man walked into his house and went straight to the kitchen". This is fine when reading to myself because as I said I can change the misread words to fit the context of the piece. However, reading "the man talked into his horse and went straight to the chicken" out loud to one's classmates was... well you can imagine what it was like for a shy pubescent schoolboy - it was mortifying.

What really did the damage though was the fact that on several occasions I was made to stand on a desk and read to the class as an example of how not to read. For me that was extremely traumatic, so much so that as a result I would often be ill in order to get out of certain lessons, or not go to school at all. I even had my appendix out at age 11 and to this day I'm not sure whether or not I really had appendicitis or if the stomach pain was psychosomatic and brought on by stress – although knowing what I know now I would put my money on the psychosomatic option. Inevitably I missed a lot of lessons which further compounded the situation.

Because of those experiences I "knew", I absolutely "knew" without any doubt, that standing up and talking in front of people was a traumatic event – how could it not be? I had learned by experience that talking in front of my peers was a traumatic, humiliating act and as such I was unable to talk in front of people - ever. This is also most likely when I developed my adoration of great entertainers – to me they were doing the equivalent of lion training, sky diving or fighting sharks. But, was it really true that talking in front of people was a traumatic event?

During my NLP training I was particularly taken by a metaphor that really struck home with me because it helped me to see the "obstacles" in my life in a completely and totally new and much more realistic way. It was part of the excellent training programme developed by Tad James the internationally acclaimed NLP and hypnotherapy trainer and the creator of Time Line Therapy. The metaphor refers to whether or not you can put something into a wheelbarrow. For example you could put this book into a wheelbarrow but you could not put writing this book into a wheelbarrow- you could even put the author into a wheelbarrow and you could even do it while he was writing this book but you still couldn't put "writing this book" into a wheelbarrow. You could put bricks and mortar in to a wheelbarrow but not building houses. You could even put planet Earth in to a wheelbarrow if it were a big enough wheelbarrow but you couldn't put life in the barrow – yes you could put living things in such as people, animals and plants in but not "life".

In all the years I've been a hypnotherapist and personal development coach, and of all the people I have worked with, including myself, not a single person has ever been able to put one of their barriers into a wheelbarrow, not a single one, providing of course that their goals were on PAR.

Let me give you some examples of the most common reasons people visit a therapist: Low self-esteem, Lack of confidence,

Addictions, Eating disorders and Phobias. Can you put any of these so called "barriers" into a wheelbarrow? No, of course not because they are not physical things, they have no structure, weight, density or volume. Sure you could put the people whose behaviour helped you develop low self-esteem or a lack of confidence into a wheelbarrow but it is your belief about yourself, because of the way in which you filtered someone else's actions or behaviour that caused the issue and you obviously can't put that in a wheelbarrow. In the same way you can put nicotine, alcohol, heroin or high sugar and high fat foods in a barrow but they are not the cause of any of the above conditions either, they are just part of the It, They, Them, That, that you give your control to.

Phobias are a fantastic example of how we unconsciously give away control and responsibility to It, They, Them, That. Imagine you have a phobia of marshmallows melted in drinking chocolate; in what way is it the marshmallows melted in drinking chocolate's fault that you have a panic attack any time someone offers you a lovely hot chocolate with melted marshmallows in it? How could marshmallows melted in drinking chocolate possibly get your heart pounding in your chest, get your adrenaline and other stress hormones pumping around your body, cause your blood pressure to drop and your breathing to increase?

OK let's imagine that for years you had suffered from the imaginary debilitating phobia of marshmallows melted in drinking chocolate that shall henceforth be known as Cocoamallowphobia. However, you have recently finished a series of hypnotherapy sessions that have allowed you to rid yourself of your debilitating Cocoamallowphobia and now you just love drinking marshmallows melted in drinking chocolate. What has changed about marshmallows melted in drinking chocolate? Absolutely nothing of course.

Now let's take this ridiculous scenario one step further and imagine that because you no longer suffer from Cocoamallowphobia you start to enjoy marshmallows melted in drinking chocolate so much that you have marshmallows melted in drinking chocolate 10 times a day. Because of your new found passion for marshmallows melted in drinking chocolate you become obese and eventually develop diabetes and fatty liver disease, and a whole host of other obesity related medical conditions; is it again the fault of the poor old marshmallows melted in drinking chocolate?

Every psychological condition I have ever worked with - from phobias to low self-esteem to eating disorders; from anxiety and stress to psychosexual and relationship problems - has been a concept, an idea based entirely on a belief, putting the sufferer under the control of It, They, Them, That. In the introduction I said "I knew I could be a Successful – I had the skills – but I also knew that no one would give me the chance to prove it" but was that really the case? What was my proof that not a single person, not one, would give me a chance?

In all probability I was made to read in front of the class by a single teacher and on only one occasion, maybe twice at the most. Yet from that I decided that all public speaking was traumatic.

"If you eat roast beef eleven times in your life, one would hardly say that person constantly eats roast beef, no it would be a rare nay freak occurrence".
Arnold J Rimmer.

People can and do spend their entire lives waiting for the opportune moment to arrive, waiting for the perfect storm, for the planets to be aligned or for the omens to be right. How many times have we heard someone say they can't lose weight because they have a slow metabolism or "I would stop smoking but I can't because my partner smokes" or any number of other similar statements. Unfortunately not only are none of these things under our control but you cannot put a single one of them into a wheelbarrow because they are all concepts. By allowing It, They, Them, That to be in control you give away all responsibility for achieving any goal. As long as you allow It, They, Them, That to be in charge, the opportune moment will never arrive.

Summary

- It, They, Them, That are psychological barriers created by our beliefs.

- If you can't put a barrier in a wheelbarrow you have given control to It, They, Them, That.

In Chapter Seven we look at how beliefs are so powerful they can create the world we experience.

Chapter Seven

Beliefs

It is our beliefs and our beliefs alone that forge the world around us. Everything we know about the world, about the people we grew up with, the people we love, the people we hate, the people we meet for the first time or those we remember from our childhoods. Every experience we have ever had or will ever have is only what we believe it to be. For example, my consulting room is a welcoming, friendly, relaxing and comfortable space, as it should be. The room is warm and has comfy chairs, it has soft low lighting, relaxing music playing and essential oil diffusers filling the room with the relaxing fragrance of sandalwood. I'm sure you can imagine the room and how it would make you feel. You may already be forming a picture of my room in your mind and in turn you may notice yourself getting a certain feeling for it simply because of how you think my room looks. You probably already have a belief about my consulting room and it makes you think of it in a certain way. Now imagine if you will, completely emptying the room. Remove everything except the walls, floor, ceiling, windows and doors. Now, place a dentist chair in the middle of the room and see sterile, clinical worktops and cupboards against the walls. What has changed about your idea of the room? Now how do you think or feel about it?

So what changed? The room is just a room, a room that you may never have seen in reality but your belief about it has changed because of your preconceptions about its use. The room itself is just a room onto which you hang your experience of it based on what you believe about it. The chances are that if you were unlucky enough to have had The Butcher of Gumsville as your childhood dentist you will have a very negative belief about the room now. On the other hand, if you have never been to the dentist as a child you will have a completely different belief about the room.

Let me give you another example. Grace came to see me some time ago for help with her fear of flying. Grace's daughter was getting married and as the mother of the bride she obviously wanted to be there for the big day. Unfortunately the marriage wasn't planned for the local chapel but instead the happy couple were jetting off to a tropical beach resort to tie the knot. Obviously this was going to be a real problem for Grace. I asked Grace what exactly was it about flying that frightened her to which she replied "everything, the whole idea of flying terrifies me". "Is the actual act of booking a holiday frightening"? I asked Grace "No, not at all" she replied "there's nothing frightening about going in to a travel agents". "What about choosing your clothes for the holiday"? I asked "No, that's not a problem – I like choosing clothes"? "How about packing your suitcase"? I asked "No I don't have a problem with that either" Grace told me. And so this went on, me asking Grace to think about each small part of the whole "flying" event until we narrowed the fear to one specific point in the journey which was the moment the aeroplane left the ground.

It turned out that Grace was convinced that the aircraft was going to blow up just as it left the ground. She could see it all happening in her mind just like watching a film. By this time Grace's belief about flying had already drastically changed from "everything, the whole idea of flying terrifies me" to a few seconds during take-off. After a little more work Grace had completely lost her fear of flying and was by this time looking forward to the experience and all because she had changed her belief about the event.

Sometime later I heard that Grace had flown and had a wonderful time at her daughter's wedding before returning to the UK and that she had actually enjoyed the experience of flying. So what had changed? Was there something different about the aeroplane? No; of course not. The aeroplane was just an aeroplane like any other aeroplane. The only thing that had changed was Grace's belief about flying. From the moment Grace was able to change her belief about flying, every time she got onto a plane, her entire world had changed. Because of a change in her belief about flying, the fear of flying or rather "It, They, Them, That" was no longer an obstacle to Grace's holidays in the sun.

Could Grace have put her obstacle in a wheelbarrow? Well she could have put the aeroplane into a wheelbarrow but she didn't have a phobia of aeroplanes – her phobia was a fear of flying and you cannot put flying into a wheelbarrow.

What was Grace's motivation when thinking about flying? Was she positively or negatively motivated? Grace's belief was that the plane was going to blow up just as it took off and that she was going to be killed in the crash. Obviously Grace was negatively motivated because she was trying "not" to think about dying and, as we shall discover later, the unconscious mind cannot processes a negative, so in reality, whenever Grace thought of flying she actually thought of dying.

The idea that by changing one's belief about an event causes our experience of that event to change in our own world obviously has profound implications for everything we do. My beliefs were that I was not academically minded and that I could not talk in front of people in a formal situation. So how did I end up as a hypnotherapist, NLP practitioner, a Personal Development Coach, and a Reiki Master/Teacher with a joint honours degree, a Master's degree and more letters after my name than you can shake a stick at? It was the change in my belief that made it possible because just like you, your friends and family and everyone else in the world, I already had all the resources I needed to achieve anything I wanted in my life so long as my goals were on PAR. The difference was that "It, They, Them, That" (in this case, my teachers from school) were no longer in control of whether or not I was academically minded, nor over my ability to talk in front of people - I was in control, I was responsible.

In other words we are the outcome of our own beliefs!

"The problem is not the problem, the problem is your attitude about the problem. Do you understand?".
Captain Jack Sparrow.

Summary

- Everything you experience is based entirely on your belief about that experience.

- By changing your belief about something you change your experience of that thing.

OK, that's all well and good but how do we get our beliefs in the first place? During the next few pages I want to show you not just how your beliefs are created but also how absolutely unique your beliefs are and therefore how equally unique your world is and your understanding of it.

Chapter Eight

The NLP Communication Model

You may not even have thought about it before today but your very first experience of the world happened even before you were born, when you were still in your mother's womb. Although it's not yet understood exactly when a foetus develops a fully working nervous system it is known that the brain, neurons and spinal cord all begin to form as early as three weeks after conception. This means that your very first experiences of the world could have happened up to eight months before you were born - even before your mother was aware she was pregnant.

We are made of an amazing community of around 15 trillion cells, all specialised to carry out specific tasks such as respiration, skeletal support, movement, metabolism and reproduction. Another part of this great community of cells are the neurons that make up an amazing sensory system that has developed through millions of years of evolution. There are many millions of these sensory nerves in our bodies allowing us to see, hear, feel, taste and smell, and each sensory system is unique to each of us which is why physically, we all experience the world around us differently; you may like hot spicy food while others find it uncomfortable and overpowering and so may prefer something a little milder in both taste and heat. I generally don't feel the cold whereas other people may never seem to get warm. So, even before we are born we are each taking in information (data) from the world around us through our custom-built sensory system and building up a unique and subjective understanding of how the world works. By the time you were born you already "knew" how the world worked. Of course you don't actually "know" how the world works; in fact as we will see, in reality we humans have a very poor understanding about the world, regardless of one's age, intelligence or education.

NLPers (as they sometimes like to be known) have a most excellent way to explain how we all develop our unique understanding of the world and how we then "re-present" our world to others as well as to ourselves. The NLP communication model was and still is one of, if not the, most important, life changing concept I have come across.

I had made real progress with regards to talking in front of people thanks to a few earlier hypnotherapy sessions, yet by the time I began studying NLP I was still only able to speak within a group. I could introduce myself, make comments and answer questions but I was still a very, very long way from being able to do these things in any sort of formal context, such as standing up in front of an audience – even an audience of only a few people. Although it didn't happen immediately the NLP communication model produced a paradigm shift in the way I thought – not just in relation to public speaking but in every aspect of my relationship with my world and most importantly of all my relationship with myself.

By understanding how I received and filtered information coming to me from the "real" real world, and how I then changed that information to fit in with my core values and beliefs to produce a unique "map" of the world according to me, I was able to change the very world in which I existed. I suddenly understood that the world I was experiencing was in fact a world that I myself was creating, second by second, and not the world as it really is. Everything I felt, every fear I had (and there were many, not just of speaking in public), my beliefs about the people I met and those I already knew and even my beliefs about who I was and how other people related to me were all based on a tiny amount of random information I had taken in and then deleted, distorted and generalised beyond all recognition.

If there is only one thing that you take from this book I hope it is a true understanding of the NLP communication model, because it explains so simply and so cleanly how we all create each and every experience in our lives, based entirely on the rules set out in the NLP Communication Model.

To fully understand this simple yet elegant model is the first step in understanding what makes us who we are and how we create the world in which we live. It also allows us to see the things we need to adjust in order to change that world.

Figure 1.

The NLP Communication Model

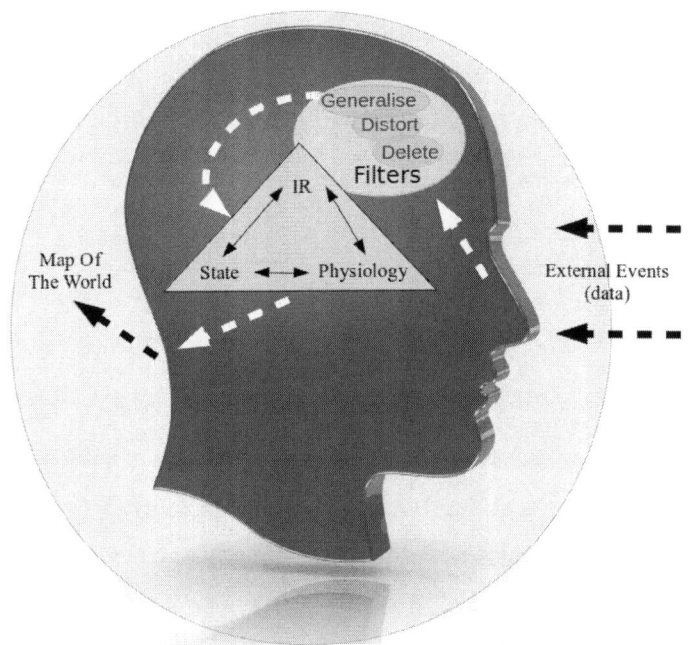

External events enter via the nervous system as randomly selected data. This data is then processed by a set of filters which delete unnecessary or unwanted information before distorting and generalising the remaining information contained in the data.

The filtered information from the external event is then adjusted according to your Internal Representation (IR), State and Physiology. This produces a map of the world which becomes your unique and subjective reality.

The NLP Communication Model shows us that what we believe to be reality is exactly that – it's what we "believe" reality to be and also why it's different, sometimes radically different to everyone else's reality.

Have you ever watched a film – let's say a comedy - with a friend and while you may have been rolling around on the floor with tears of laughter pouring down your face, your friend may have been looking at you as though you had gone mad because they just didn't find the film at all funny. My wife enjoys watching psychological horror films but if I'm totally honest they frighten the shit out of me! How can this be? You and your friend, me and my wife, we are given the same information (data) and yet we produce completely different responses to it. The reason is explained beautifully by the NLP Communication Model.

Filtering

As I said we have millions of sensory receptors and they allow us to monitor both our internal and external environments. Once this data has entered through our sensory network it is then subjected to a filtering system which is totally unique to each of us. These filters delete, distort and generalise the information before it's moulded by our state and our physiology. Although sources differ on the exact amount it's believed that there are around 2 million bits of information available to us every second of every day throughout our entire lives. However it's also thought by the boffins who study such things that we are only capable of taking in or handling around 124 bits of information every second. Now let's just put that into some kind of perspective. If you only take in 124 bits of data out of the 2,000,000 bits of data available to you, that means that you only ever take in a tiny 0.01% of anything that happens to you or has ever happened to you every second of every day. Or to turn it around, you miss around 99.99% of everything that ever happens in your life – that is immense!

Your sensory system is totally unique to you and as such you will randomly select a unique 124 bits of information every second – so what are the chances that two people experiencing the same event, at the same time, are actually taking in the same 124 bits of information every second? It's so improbable it's almost impossible.

Once this tiny amount of randomly selected information has entered your sensory system you then delete, distort and generalise it to within a nanometre of its life.

Deletion

If you were to ask someone who lives in a fairly average town-house on a fairly average street to tell you how many lamp posts or blue cars or green doors there are in their street, they probably would not be able to tell you. Although they may have lived on the same street for many years they would be unlikely to know the answer, yet they will have seen the lamp posts, blue cars and green doors on hundreds if not thousands of occasions.

The last time you drove a car, how many people did you see walking a dog; how many crossed the road in front of you? How many cars in front of you braked without indicating before turning? You probably have no idea. Hopefully the dog walkers and the careless driving of those inconsiderate motorists didn't cause you to have an accident, and you're not actually reading this book from a hospital bed. And yet despite the fact that you didn't run over the dog walkers or drive into the back of the careless drivers there is a very good chance that you don't remember them. This is because your unconscious mind decides that this information is not important enough for you to keep in your memory and so it deletes it. Imagine what would happen if you retained every piece of information you ever took in? Your head would be so full of lamp posts and blue cars and green doors and dog walkers and inconsiderate motorists that it would take forever for you to recall anything, if at all. Deletion means that unlike an old hard drive that is so full of files it gets slower and slower, you don't have to keep defragging your mind.

I have a notion that this is where we get the effect of negative hallucinations from too. A negative hallucination is the opposite of a hallucination. During a negative hallucination you can't see something even if it is right in front of you; the best known and most common example of a negative hallucination is when you can't find your car keys. You are so busy telling yourself that you can't find them, that even your unconscious starts to believe it (you cannot not think of something) and so it decides it's not worth keeping any information about your keys if you already know they aren't there, and simply deletes it.

Distortion

So after randomly taking in a tiny 0.01% of all the information available to you every second of your life and then deleting most of that because it's of no use to you, you now distort the even smaller fraction of data to fit in with what you already "know" to be true based on your core values and beliefs.

When I was 14 years old, if I wasn't breaking bits off my body by trying stupid stunts on my skateboard, I was training to become a rock star (I'm still training to be a rock star by the way).

My weapon of choice for this noble cause was and still is the axe, or the guitar as it's sometimes known, and like all trainee rock stars when I was 14 years old, "the" piece of music one had to learn to play was Stairway to Heaven by Led Zeppelin. Having achieved this noble goal the next step was to play Stairway To Heaven at "the" holiest of holy festivals, Glastonbury. Now, depending on your age and musical taste, you may or may not remember that several years ago Rolf Harris brought out a cover version of Stairway To Heaven, and if you have similar beliefs to me regarding this piece of rock history you will have been totally mortified, just as I was. In my opinion, based on my core values and beliefs, the bearded Aussie player of wobble-boards and painter of pictures should have gone nowhere near such a holy rock anthem. Then....! Then.....! To make matters worse – to rub salt into my already mortally wounded belief system, he only went and played it at Glastonbury – the holiest of holy venues.

Now, like any other mature, self-respecting middle-aged British male who has been upset by someone, I went straight to my mum and told her about it. That was a big mistake. Although my mum and I are quite close, she does not exactly share my taste in music - probably due to the hours and hours of excruciating pain she had to endure while I was learning to play the guitar (a role now undertaken by my wife) and more specifically Stairway To Heaven. This is what she said when I told her of Rolf's heresy "Oh I like Rolf Harris, he's probably turned a really noisy heavy metal song in to a nice tune"! Yes it still hurts even to this day but I'm working on it – luckily I know a very good therapist.

So how did two people who are as close as me and my mum take the same information and come away with two completely opposite views? The answer is that we both took a random fraction of the information available to us, deleted what was of no use and then distorted what was left to fit in with our core values and beliefs - what we already knew to be true - and arrived at two opposing views regarding Rolf Harris' cover of Stairway to Heaven.

I must point out that until recently I had nothing but the greatest respect and admiration for Rolf Harris as a painter and children's entertainer, in fact despite recent events, I still consider him to be a wonderful part of my childhood having watched with amazement many times as he produced fantastic paintings by simply slapping some paint onto a wall.

However, I now have another belief about Rolf Harris based on his conviction as a sex offender and it seems I'm not alone. Since his conviction the value of his art work has dropped considerably and yet in reality what has changed about his paintings? Nothing, they are just paintings. It is people's beliefs about him as a person that has changed their belief about the value of his art work. Think of it this way, instead of being an artist, if Rolf Harris had been a surgeon performing ground-breaking and life saving open-heart surgery would his work be of less value now than it was prior to his conviction? It was something of a coincidence that the case against Rolf Harris began just after I had written this section of the book and following his conviction I considered omitting the whole section. However, on reflection I realised that Rolf Harris' conviction was a perfect example of how the way we filter information has a massive effect on our beliefs and in turn on the world that we experience.

We are constantly reminded on the news of the conflict between the Palestinians and the Israelis but what do you think would happen if a group of children from each side of the conflict were taken as babies and brought up without any knowledge of the conflict? What would they think of each other? Would there even be a distinction between them? No, their beliefs would be based on the information they filtered which would not have included anything about any conflict other than the usual conflicts associated with children as they grow up together.

Generalisation

After missing 99.99% of everything and then deleting most of what's left and then distorting that tiny bit of data to fit in with your core values and beliefs you still haven't finished. You also generalise everything.

Imagine you go to visit a friend at their house and they have some new chairs – let's say they're Poangs. If you have never seen a Poang before, or not even a chair that looked like a poang, you would still know they were chairs. You would not need to learn "chair" all over again to incorporate a new style that you hadn't seen before. In the same way most people haven't driven a tank, but if they have a driving licence they would be able to learn to drive a tank by generalising. They already know what acceleration and breaking are and how to turn left and right and gears and reverse and so on. It would take them a while to get to grips with the mechanics of driving a tank but in general they would already know much of it.

Imagine if every time you met someone new you had to learn "face" all over again. People's faces can vary greatly from the colour of their hair, skin and eyes to the shape of their face, mouth nose etc. and yet even though you may not know the person you are looking at, you do recognise they have a face. Generalising like this makes it much easier and quicker for us to begin to recognise people – this person has a face, their skin is this colour, their hair is that colour and that length, their eyes are that colour and shape etc. until generally a person with all these general features is Bob - "hello Bob".

By adding the finer details we move from recognising someone as a person to, a person I may know, to a person I do know, to that person I do know.

Generalisation allows us to understand, recognise and utilise things without having to re-learn everything from scratch – it gives us the ability to learn quickly – but not necessarily accurately. Generalisations give an evolutionary edge over other species, as it allows for much faster decision making at times of danger or opportunity. For example, a man being chased by a lion does not really need to know which lion it is, or even if it's male, female, young or old. He doesn't even need to know if it is in fact a lion because detail is not important at that moment – just the fact that it is a big cat and it wants to eat him is all he needs to worry about.

"All generalizations are false, including this one".
Mark Twain.

Internal Representation

Once you've randomly taken in a fraction of the data available to you and then deleted, distorted and generalised what's left to within a nanometre of its life, this makes up part of your internal representation (IR). Even now you still haven't got your finished reality because your internal representation is also affected by both your state (are you happy, sad, anxious, frightened or excited etc.) and your physiology (are you well or ill, hot or cold etc.).

Imagine you are in bed suffering from the UK's favourite winter bug, the Noro Virus, and let's add a bout of diarrhoea for good measure. Your best friend decides to pop around and tell you his best joke in an effort to try and cheer you up - how funny do you think the joke would be? Not very, I would suggest! Now imagine you are perfectly well and happy, you've been out with your friends and had a great time and maybe the odd glass of vino tinto, your friend tells you exactly the same, lame joke but this time you may wet yourself laughing! Why? What was different about the joke? Obviously there was nothing different about the joke – it was in fact your whole world that was different. Your state and physiology have a massive influence over your interpretation of the information you receive via your nervous system.

Maps

Once you have your internal representation of the world and it has been adjusted or affected by your state and your physiology you then cast that out into the real world and that is how the world works according to you right at that moment – this is your "map" of the world and it is totally subjective and completely unique to you, and you do this every second of every day of your life.

You take in a phenomenally small amount of random information, delete, distort and generalise it and this in turn is affected by your state and your physiology. You then cast this out into..... the...... well, the out there into whatever reality really is, as your map of the world and of course, everyone else is doing exactly the same thing - producing their very own maps of the world and casting them out there.

I believe the late and very great Douglas Adams must have understood this concept perfectly when he wrote:-

"You cannot see what I see because you see what you see. You cannot know what I know because you know what you know. What I see and what I know cannot be added to what you see and what you know because they are not the same kind. Neither can it replace what I see and what I know, because that would be to replace you yourself".
Douglas Adams, Mostly Harmless.

What Is This Reality Thing Anyway?

Another fun little NLP quote is, "perception is projection", which makes complete sense if you have really firmly grasped the concept of the NLP Communication Model. Perception is projection suggests that everything we experience is only what we projected onto the world - what we perceive as "real" is almost entirely what we put there in the first place. As John Lennon once said "Reality leaves a lot to the imagination". I would go even further and suggest that our reality leaves everything to the imagination - or at least 99.99% of everything.

Reality is like watching a film; what we believe we are seeing is a constant or analogue flow of movement. For example if you watch a film of a diver leaping from a high board and gracefully delivering several elegant acrobatic movements before disappearing in to the water without so much as a splash, you believe you are watching the whole event but in reality you only see a series of still photographs that are shown in rapid succession and your mind fills in the missing parts.

So you can see that what you know about the world, or what you "believe" you know about the world is completely unique to you.

Feedback

This leads us nicely on to the subject of feedback. In Chapter two I introduced the concept of feedback and when you think about it, given that everything we experience about the world is only what we created (perception is projection) in the first place, then it makes sense that everything we experience is in fact feedback.

I tend to divide feedback in to two categories which are internal feedback and external feedback. Internal feedback is how we evaluate our own actions based on how we believe we are doing at any one time – "am I communicating well today?", "how am I treating my loved ones?", "am I happy?" etc. External feedback is how we interpret other people's actions and comments in relation to our behaviour.

A good example of internal and external feedback at work would be Jane's story in Chapter Five. While getting ready for her night out with her best friend and the chance of meeting up with a man from work, Jane would have tried on several outfits, she would have done her hair and put on make-up. Only when her internal feedback told her she looked right was she happy to go out. Next, the external feedback she received from Emily backed up her own internal feedback about how she looked. However the external feedback she got from Mr Right was the complete opposite of her internal feedback. When asked "when is your baby due" Jane's filter system kicked in and all she heard was "I think you are really fat" from Mr Right, but worse and even more damaging was the fact that Jane distorted this to also mean that her friend Emily had purposefully not told her how she really looked in order to make herself look better when they were out together, when in reality (whatever that may be), Emily was trying not to hurt Jane and Mr Right honestly thought Jane was pregnant and this of course has no bearing on whether or not he found her attractive.

This is really important to keep in mind when receiving feedback from someone. It doesn't matter how negative or positive that feedback seems to you because it is only what it is because of how you filter the information. For example if you were to ask two people, one who you like and the other whom you dislike, to give you feedback about how you look right now what do you think their feedback would be like?

Even if they were both to give you negative feedback which one are you likely to consider the harshest?

It's also important to keep in mind that the person giving you feedback has interpreted your actions, or in the case of Jane, her appearance, according to their own subjective map of the world, which is of course a product of their own filtering system

I always felt hard done by when receiving feedback from my parents with regard to my early years as a trainee rock star. The fact is that I didn't like their feedback because they weren't telling me what I wanted to hear – usually what they were telling me was "turn it down". I felt they were being unfair and I took it personally. In reality that was my fault not theirs. Their feedback was honest and based on the undeniable truth that both of my parents massively disliked rock music and as such it wouldn't have mattered if I could have played like Hendrix himself, they still would not have liked it. So when I played them something I'd just learned and asked them what they thought of it, if they said it was "too loud" and "don't you know anything by Val Doonican", they were being honest.

Summary

- The NLP Model explains how information is filtered and then altered before representing your own reality.

- Deletion – information not considered important is deleted.

- Distortion – you distort information from your senses to fit in with your core values and beliefs or what you already "know" to be true.

- Generalisation – Information is generalised in order to speed up learning and recognition.

- Internal Representation – After incoming information has been deleted, distorted and generalised it is then adjusted according to your state and physiology to form your internal representation of the world.

- Maps – Your internal representation is projected on to the real world to form your own unique "map" of the world according to you at any given time.

- Perception is Projection – the world you experience is created by you and projected on to the real world.

Feedback

Internal feedback is a system used to monitor your own actions based on how you believe you are doing at any one time. External Feedback is a way of monitoring other people's belief about you at any one time.

In the next chapter we are going to look at who you think you are and your place in the world. I will also introduce the idea of the Self-ish triangle.

Chapter 9

Whose Life is it Anyway?

On the whole we human beings are like most other primates in that we are naturally gregarious creatures. We possess the amazing ability to build incredibly complex relationships with many other people (and other animals, and plants, even inanimate objects), all of whom will have their own unique set of beliefs and values (not the plants and inanimate objects of course - except perhaps to some "special" people). Some of their beliefs and values may even be at complete odds with our own. They will be experiencing their world according to their unique map and yet we are still able to interact with them and for the most part, live harmoniously together for the benefit of all within our community or social group. Even the most resolute loner or the most anti-social, grumpy old git will have some order of relationships and preferred acquaintances. In fact, very few people choose to cut themselves off completely from the world around them, and in our modern society it is virtually impossible to do so even if one wanted to.

"It's all for the greater good", "The greater good". Neighbourhood Watch Alliance (NWA).

Within these relationships most people will spend at least a part of their life looking after one or more other person or persons. Some may spend all of their time either looking after, or trying to care for other people, be they family members such as children, a partner, a friend or people they may not even know but have volunteered to help. The reasons why we help others can be many and varied, such as looking after an elderly parent out of love or just because of the family bond, or helping out in the community simply out of altruism. Many people including nurses, doctors, home helpers, carers and yes, even therapists, earn their living by helping others, while some people completely miss out on earning a living at all because they give up all of their time to help others.

Whatever your particular relationships with those around you, whether you have a huge matrix of friends, family and colleagues or just one or two people you deal with out of necessity, you will inevitably have a preference for some over others, for whatever reasons. So here's another question I often ask my clients: "Out of everybody you know, who are the most important people in your life right now"?

Exercise 3.

Think of the most important people in your life right now and in the column entitled "Who" in Table 4 write their names in order of importance to you.

NB: If possible do this before moving on to the next part of this section!

Table 4.

The Most Important People In My Life Right Now.

Who	Relationship	Reason

Something I've noticed over the years is that clients will often tell me the names of the people they "think" should be the most important in their lives, or more likely who they think "I" think should be the most important people in their lives rather than those who actually are most important to them. So, please be honest with yourself and if that is what you have done here it's time to change the names to only the people who "are" genuinely important in your life right now. In the "Relationship" column write down that person's relationship to you and finally, in the "Reason" column enter a few words that explain why they are important to you.

The Self-ish Triangle

Often-times people will use the terms self-esteem, self-worth and self-confidence interchangeably but they are not the same thing at all and each will have a different effect on our lives.

Like your internal representation, state and physiology, self-esteem, self-worth and self-confidence make up another internal love triangle or the Self-ish Triangle as I like to think of it.

Figure 2
The Self-ish Triangle

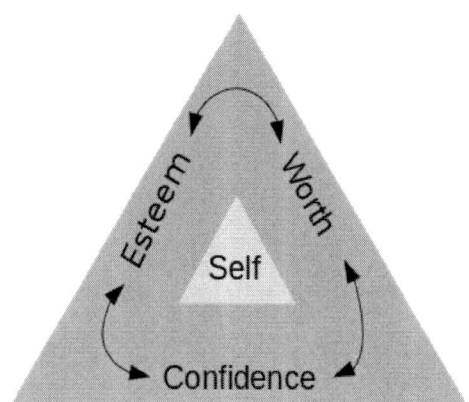

However, unlike the triangle that creates your map of the world, if one side of this triangle changes it does not always affect the other two sides.

Self-Esteem

Self-esteem is a very temporal, flighty little creature that can change it's mind in a heartbeat. Your self-esteem is based on your belief about how you are doing in the here and now – have you just done something you feel really proud of or completely ashamed of for example. Your self-esteem can be shattered in an instant by someone telling you that you have done a bad job when you thought you'd done something really well, or by a harsh comment (perceived or real) from a friend or peer about how you look.

"Ah smug mode".
Kryten, Red Dwarf

On a positive note though, one's self-esteem can go up just as fast as it can come down. For example if someone you look up to and admire tells you how well you are doing, or you are told how good you look in a new outfit you will more than likely feel a sense of achievement. You may feel pride growing in your chest, you'll stand up straighter, hold your head up, look people in the eye and enter what I like to call "smug mode". So our self-esteem is directly related to how well we think we are doing and what we believe others think about how we are doing at any one time.

Sometimes even the simplest thing such as a completely innocent comment or remark can send our self-esteem soaring into the stratosphere or crashing to the ground in a ball of metaphorical flames.

Self-Worth

Unlike self-esteem, your self-worth is a much more stable, long-term part of your make-up based on your belief about how valuable you are – what you feel you are worth as an individual. If they suffer from low self-worth even the most successful of people can and do question whether they deserve the things or the lifestyle they may have – "should I really be in such a great relationship" or "do I deserve to have this lovely house" or "I'm not worthy of having the job I've always wanted". In fact I wonder if this could be one of the reasons why so many successful film stars, rock stars and other top professionals end up in therapy - on the one hand they are extremely gifted actors, singers, musicians etc. bursting with oodles of ability and confidence whilst on the other they feel unable to accept the life they have and the accolades they achieve because they believe they do not deserve them.

A lack of self-worth can be extremely destructive even in people with high self-esteem and an abundance of self-confidence in their own abilities. No matter what a person knows they are capable of, no matter how well they think they are doing, if they do not feel they are worthy of having the things they desire they will often sabotage their own chances of getting them. Self-sabotage is responsible for the destruction of many a career, great friendships, loving relationships, further education and personal development etc. Perhaps you know someone who constantly finds reasons to end perfectly good relationships, or messes up every job interview they attend even though they are the best candidate for that particular vacancy – perhaps that person is you? The good news is that like everything in your map of the world, your sense of self-worth is based entirely on beliefs you developed as a child and like all beliefs they can be changed.

Self-Confidence

I always think that this is the most fickle of the three sides of the Self-ish Triangle as it can be both temporal and long-term and different for different situations and events. For example you may be really confident at a particular sport but not at all confident in a social situation. I've often wondered if we are good at some things because we are confident in our ability to do them or if we are confident in our ability to do them because we are good at those things – I'm sure someone will have studied that question! You may be the best, most gifted person at your job and yet you never give it your best shot because of a lack of confidence in your own abilities. Have you ever heard someone singing beautifully as they potter around the house or take a shower and yet that same person may have a weak shaky voice if asked to sing in public.

Confidence tricksters for example work entirely on their confidence in order to gain your confidence – the clue is in the name! They rip us off by gaining our confidence but they could never do that if they did not have confidence in their own ability to deceive us. However, I would hazard a guess that because of the nature of their work, confidence tricksters may also have very low self-esteem and/or self-worth.

Just because someone can do something really well it doesn't automatically mean they believe in their ability to do it or that they feel they deserve any reward they may earn for their efforts.

Over confidence can also be an issue if say, your confidence in your own ability far exceeds your capability. Imagine for a moment if you believed you are the greatest boxer that ever lived but in actual fact, far from floating like a butterfly and stinging like a bee, you float like a breeze block and sting like a Johnson's cotton bud. As a consequence, you are likely to have been knocked over more times than a pub skittle, so it's not just your face that takes a beating at every fight but your self-esteem is likely to go home with two black eyes and a broken nose too.

For as long as I can remember I have been a fan of Formula 1 motor racing. I know that Formula 1 in particular is a bit of a Marmite sport but I love it for many different reasons including the technology, the glamour, the speed and noise of the cars and the bravery and skill of the drivers. Obviously all of the drivers are extremely talented and have an abundance of natural ability, but I believe that what makes the difference between being world champion and being one of the other drivers is having just the right amount of confidence in your ability and in the capability of the car. Too little confidence and the driver will not get the best from the car; too much and there is likely to be a crash but when all else is equal it is the driver with exactly the right amount of confidence that will get 100% from himself and from the car and go on to win more races than any other contenders and therefore take the championship.

Over the last several years I've been lucky enough to work with many amazing clients from all over the UK and presenting a wide variety of conditions. Some of the most frequently presented problems I encounter are issues such as guilt, social and sexual relationship issues, performance anxiety, career and relationship self-sabotage amongst others. The thing all of these issues have in common is that they are caused by one or more of the Self-ish triangle issues of low self-worth, low self-esteem and low self-confidence which of course are all based entirely on false beliefs developed as we move through life. After all, a baby is born with no concept of its own value, or abilities or any knowledge of how well it's doing – these are things it has to learn and develop over time.

OK, so looking at your list of VIPs in Table 4, where did you place yourself on the list? Did you even include yourself? How long would your list need to be before your name is on it?

There are many reasons why a person may experience issues relating to the Self-ish triangle, far too many to cover in this book but as I mentioned they are all based on false beliefs developed over time - but whatever the cause, the chances are the last person on their list of important people will be themselves – that's if they put themselves on the list at all.

Summary

- The Self-ish Triangle consists of your self-esteem, self-worth and self-confidence.
- Self-esteem is a very temporal and based on your belief about how you are doing in the here and now.
- Self-worth is more stable and based on your belief about how valuable you are – what you feel you are worth as an individual.
- Self-confidence can be both temporary and long-term and different for different situations and events.

In the next chapter we will look at why it is so important that you put yourself at the centre of your world.

Chapter 10

The Centre Of The Known Universe

Here's another two of my favourite questions that I like to present to clients "Should you be the most important person in your life"? And if so, Why aren't you the most important person in your life"?

When I suggest to someone that they should be the most important person in their own life their initial reaction is usually one of shock. They often say things like "my children are so much more important than me" or "what about my partner"? They feel that being the most important person in their own life is somehow selfish, that it's everyone else who should be more important – but can that really be true? Is it really selfish, arrogant or self-centred to be the most important person in your own life?

Have you ever travelled on an aeroplane? If so you will most likely remember that moment as the plane is taxiing down the runway when the cabin crew do the obligatory safety talk. That's usually the time most people reach for the in-flight magazine, bury their heads in some mind-numbing story about wine production in the French Pyrenees and try their hardest not to listen. After all, the last thing one wants to think about just before take-off is the idea that the plane could possibly crash.

Well whether you took any notice of it or not, there is a point in the safety demonstration when you're told that in the event of a sudden decrease in cabin pressure, an oxygen mask will automatically drop from an overhead compartment and that you must put your own mask on before helping anyone else. There is of course a very good reason for doing this. Apart from being very social animals, we also share another trait with our primate relatives, in fact we share this trait with almost all other forms of life, and that is our fondness for oxygen. I'm sure you know that in the absence of oxygen we humans have a tendency to pass out fairly quickly. This is usually followed quite closely by death, so if you are busy trying to help the person next to you put their mask on, there is a very good chance that you and the person you're helping are both going to pass out and probably die. Now imagine if this scenario were taking place in the cockpit! Both pilots trying to help each other on with their oxygen masks and so both pass out and.... ahhhhhhh – KERSPLAT

In the event of a sudden drop in cabin pressure at 38 thousand feet, who do you think is "the" single most important person on that aeroplane? If you said the pilot you'd be wrong.... yes, yes, I realise that without the pilot the plane is going to crash but please let me finish... you would also be right. As far as the pilot is concerned, as far as his responsibility to the passengers and crew goes, he needs to be the best that he can be to have the greatest chance of landing the plane safely and saving the lives of all those on board. As a side effect he is likely to become a national hero, write a best-selling book and sell the film rights for a small, or even large, fortune.

The important thing to remember about our brave captain is that he needed to be the best that he could be for himself first,

He needed to be "the" most important person in his own world first and as a consequence he was the best he could be for everyone else on the plane. Imagine if your pilot was suffering from extremely low self-esteem, his self-worth was shot to pieces and his self-confidence was at an all time low, just at the moment he, you and everyone else on the plane needed all three parts of his self-ish triangle to be at their absolute all-time very best. What if there was a problem with the plane and instead of doing his utmost to save the lives of himself and everyone else on board, instead of thinking "I want to live, I deserve to live and I know I can land this plane and save the lives of all the passengers and crew" he actually thought "oh what's the point, I don't deserve to live and I'm never going to land this bloody plane safely anyway"? No, the best scenario for everyone on board that plane is that according to his own map of the world the pilot is "the" single most important person in his world so that in the event of an emergency he and everyone else on board will have the best chance of survival.

It is exactly the same for you in your seat on that plane at that moment – yes the pilot is important but whether or not he lands the plane safely is not under your control. The only thing that is under your control is you and the decisions you make. Imagine that the pilot was the best he could be because he was "the" most important person in his world and so he landed the plane safely. Unfortunately although almost everyone else on board survived the sudden drop in cabin pressure and therefore a lack of oxygen, and the ensuing emergency descent and landing, a mother and father and their two children suffocated because the parents had passed out while trying to put the oxygen masks on the children before taking care of themselves. Had the parents put the masks on themselves first as instructed to do so by the cabin crew during the safety talk, they would then have both survived and been able to save the children.

Now, do you think it is a selfish act for a pilot to be the most important person in his own life? I certainly don't. Should he take care of his own health and well-being before that of his family, friends, passengers and crew? Absobloodylutely - I for one want my pilot to be in the best physical and psychological condition possible because that will give me the best chance of survival should a problem arise.

In your own map of the world, far from being selfish, being "the" most important person in the world is imperative for everyone else in your life – for you to be the best that you can be for those around you; you first have to be the best that you can be for you.

Like many people I believed that low self-esteem, lack of self-worth and low self-confidence was the meat and potatoes of the young – particularly teens! However, since becoming a therapist I've been surprised to find that many clients presenting these issues are mature; often coming up to or recently past retirement age. This can be a time of massive upheaval, a time for a wholesale re-evaluation of ones life - the kids have grown up and moved away and now have their own lives and children of their own. Sometimes they begin questioning the relationship they have with their partner now that the kids are gone – do they really love their partner or were they together for the sake of the children? Perhaps they have become recently widowed and, having lived for their children, their partner or their relationship for most of their lives they suddenly have no goal, no direction. Many who find themselves in this situation will begin to question who they are. Having lived for others for so long they suddenly realise they have no life of their own and never have. Now, without anyone else to look after, they realise they have no idea who they are or what they want to do. After a lifetime of looking after others, of being needed, of having a purpose in life, people can suddenly find their reason for being has gone. Having spent all their time trying to be everything to everyone instead of the best they could be for themselves first, they were ironically not being the best they could be for anyone.

"I feel thin, sort of stretched, like butter scraped over too much bread".
Bilbo Baggins.

For anyone having issues relating to the Self-ish triangle the most important thing to realise is that right now is the time to put your own oxygen mask on – now is the time to start becoming the best that you can be for you. Only then will you also be the best for everyone else in your life.

Summary

- By being the most important person in your own life you can become the best that you can be.

- When you become the best you can be for you, you also become the best you can be for everyone else.

- Now is the time to put your own oxygen mask on and become the best you can be..... for you!

In Part Three we will look at how you can use your new-found understanding of you and your world to move forward – towards your goal.

Part 3

Getting It

Chapter 11

It's The Strategy - Stupid

As we have seen, whenever we do anything at all we must first be motivated in order for us to act, and it's our thoughts, both conscious and unconscious, that produce the drivers for our motivation. But it's the strategies we use that produce our behaviour and inevitably determine whether or not our outcome is positive or negative.

Strategies

A strategy is simply a sequence of steps that we run unconsciously which produces an outcome in the form of a behaviour. Problems arise however when we run ineffective strategies or strategies that are completely wrong for a particular situation. Even great strategies when used in the wrong place or at the wrong time will cause problems. It's like a computer programme where the strategies would be the sub routines that are run within the programme. Have you ever found yourself doing something and continually getting the same result – the wrong result? No matter how hard you try or what new tactic you use you always end up with the same result – the wrong result. Perhaps your relationships always end the same way or your opinion is always taken the wrong way by others. Perhaps you are really enthusiastic about new projects but you never seem to finish anything you start, or you continually underachieve at a sport that you know you are more than capable of excelling at.

Panic attacks are excellent examples of good strategies being run at the wrong time or for the wrong reason. If you happen to be out walking in the countryside and you are suddenly confronted by a very large, very hungry and very angry grizzly bear, then suddenly receiving a massive burst of adrenaline is a totally natural response. Running a sequence of steps that will prepare your mind and body to either fight or run for your life from a very large, very hungry and very angry grizzly bear is a great strategy. Unfortunately, running that same strategy whilst relaxing on the beach during your family holiday is never going to end well.

I have deliberately made an effort to keep this book light so I'm not going to delve any deeper into strategies – perhaps that will be for another book. In this respect I'd like to use an analogy to explain strategies the way I understand them.

You Are The Architect

Imagine you decide to sign up to a university degree to study architecture. On day one you find yourself in a room taking part in your first practical lesson with other architectural students from all over the world. You are all allowed to choose from a large selection of materials and told you have two hours to design and build a scale model of some form of residential housing. At the end of the allotted time you are all told to take your finished models and place them on a large table at the front of the classroom. What do you think would be the first thing you would notice about the models?

I think the first and most noticeable thing would be that every model looks very different from every other model. In fact some of the models are nothing like each other, some are blocks of flats, some are single story buildings, others are ultra-modern while some look very traditional and reflect the culture of the community from which the student who made it came. Why would this be? All the students had the same resources in terms of mental and technical abilities and they all had exactly the same materials to choose from and yet the models they created were all so different. The reason is simple, it's the materials that are chosen at the start and the way in which they are put together that produce the finished building.

In the building analogy above, your goal is your own architectural drawing that you must work from – it's the bigger picture. Your thoughts are the raw materials you choose to make your model and the strategies are the way in which they are combined. The finished model is your outcome or behaviour.

So you can see that once you have your architectural drawing (your goal) if you then choose the wrong materials (thoughts) for the job, it doesn't matter how well or in what order they are combined (the strategy), it will never produce the right model (outcome) as described in your drawing.

When building a house, in order to end up with a building that matches the original architect's design you must choose the right materials to begin with and combine them in the correct order.

When it comes to people becoming the best that they can be – surely the essence of all personal development – it's simply a no-brainer that the most effective strategies must be discovered and put into place. Not only do we need the right strategies but they need to be implemented in the correct sequence.

Re-framing

Most of the time our "intended" outcomes are positive but as we now know, it's our motivation that will affect our goals and inevitably determine whether or not the outcome we actually end up with is positive or negative. It's not the intention behind the goal but the motivation that's the issue and this can be easily changed by a simple tool known as re-framing.

Re-framing your goals gives you an easy way to run much more efficient strategies because it allows you to utilise the necessary thoughts, so that the correct actions are put into operation in the correct sequence.

In Table 5 below I have re-framed the goals in Table 2 so that they are now positively motivated and you can see how the outcomes have changed from negative to positive.

Table 5.

Re-framed Table of Goal – Motivation – Outcome

Goal	Motivation	Outcome
To get a better job	Better working conditions, more money, more free time	New job with higher status, better conditions, more money, less hours .
Become healthier	Better health, increase self-esteem, live longer, be more active	Become slimmer, feel fitter, increased confidence/self-esteem

Exercise 3.

Look again at your answers in Table 1 (Chapter 1) and think about how you can re-frame them to be positively motivated and therefore produce positive goals. This will lead you to thoughts that produce the right strategies to move towards positive outcomes.

In Table 6 below write your new goals in the "What Do You Want" column, and what you now believe is stopping you from achieving them in the "What Stops You From Getting It" column.

Table 6.

Re-Framed Table of What Do You Want vs What Stops You From Getting It.

What Do You Want?	What Stops You Getting It?

NB: Remember that your goals must be stated in the positive, they must be physically achievable and they must be realistic - on PAR.

Summary

- A strategy is an unconscious sequence of steps which produce an outcome.
- Even a great strategy will produce a negative outcome if used at the wrong time or for the wrong event.
- Re-framing allows you to change negative motivation to positive motivation.
- By re-framing negatively motivated goals to positively motivated goals, a strategy can be adjusted to one that produces a positive outcome.

In the next chapter we find out why we don't always get what we want because our unconscious minds cannot "not" think of something.

Chapter 13

You Cannot NOT Think Of Something

Don't Think Of A Tree

It is absolutely crucial that we understand why the way that we think will have a direct effect on whether we get what we want or whether we get what we don't want. As I may have mentioned once or twice already, this is not meant to be an NLP text book or training manual but many of the ideas presented here are based around NLP concepts and one of the fundamental concepts of NLP is that the unconscious mind cannot process a negative.

Although you may not always be aware of it, your unconscious mind processes your thoughts as pictures and because your unconscious mind sees pictures of the things you think about, whether you want to think of a particular thing or if you don't want to think of a particular thing you will inevitably generate a picture of it. In other words we have to think about the thing we may or may not want to think of in order to know what it is that we may or may not want to think of.

Need proof? OK let me use a classic NLP example, "Don't think of a tree".

Did you think of a tree? OK let's try even harder not to think of a tree – really concentrate on not thinking of that tree with its tall, thick trunk, strong branches and lush green leaves. OK now, don't make it a blue tree – really focus hard on not making that tree with it's tall trunk and strong branches have bright blue leaves. Now, don't think of putting an elephant in the tree. You can choose any colour elephant that you don't want to put in that blue tree but whatever you do, if it's not already, please, please, please don't make the elephant pink.

So, it really doesn't matter what you are thinking of; whether it's something you want or something you don't want, your unconscious mind will always generate the picture of it even though for most of the time you are unaware of it happening. This is how your unconscious mind "codes" your thoughts.

Because it's your unconscious mind that produces your behaviour, having an unconscious mind that only codes thoughts in pictures and as such cannot process a negative, is something of a double-edged sword.

On the positive side, the benefit of an unconscious mind coding your thoughts in picture form is that you are able to react to many situations instantly, without the need to think – a valuable resource for survival if you need to act fast, such as escaping from a predator or jumping out of the way of a speeding car. The trouble is that the unconscious mind cannot distinguish between the things we want and those we don't want. It has no concept of reality, time and space, desire, fear or long-term goals - it just sees the pictures of the things we are thinking of and we take action accordingly at an unconscious level. In times of danger, in life or death situations when your ability to act quickly is crucial, such as jumping out of the way of a car, waking up to find the house on fire or suddenly being attacked by a three headed dog (did you see a three headed dog?), there is no need to worry about whether your motivation is positive or negative, whether your clothes look good or even if you're naked. The fact is that when your life is in danger, where you are at that time is not a healthy environment to hang around in. In fact, anywhere else is likely to be a hell of a lot safer than where you are, and so your unconscious mind will produce the necessary behaviour to change the situation and hopefully move you away from danger.

It's only your conscious mind that can see the value of any given thing or situation, work out the pros and cons for each event and come up with a logical strategy. When your unconscious mind produces the picture of the thing you're thinking of (whether you want it or not), it will trigger a series of strategies that produce a behavioural response. For example, if you have a phobia of spiders and you are shown a photo of a spider you may scream, your heart may start to beat faster and you might begin to breathe more quickly. Even though you know "logically" that you are perfectly safe because it is only a photograph of a spider, you are still likely to have a negative physical response. Even if there is no photograph involved and someone is asked "not" to think of the thing they have a phobia of they are still likely to have the same phobic reaction.

If you were ever unlucky enough to be attacked by a three headed dog, or if you were to step out in front of a speeding car, the chances are your unconscious mind wouldn't see a picture of you being attacked or hit by the car but rather a picture of you running away and hiding or jumping out of the way. If that means jumping over a wall then so be it. You do not stop to think about what might be on the other side of the wall, such as a long drop or a main road – even worse it could be the garden from which the three headed dog escaped and where its mum and dad and brothers and sisters live, or perhaps a six lane motorway. In such a situation there is no time for logical thought – move or be attacked – move or be run over - ergo you move.

I remember many years ago riding my motorbike along the A470 near Cardiff during the evening rush hour. Anyone who commutes along the A470 will know that it can be an extremely fast and busy road with many heavy goods vehicles moving between the South Wales valleys and Cardiff and the M4. It was a very hot day (yes they do happen even in South

Wales) and the traffic was heavy so I opened my visor to get some cool air. A few minutes later, somewhere around the turn-off for Treforest, a lovely big bumble bee flew right through the gap in my visor and into my crash helmet. Well, things became very exciting very quickly I can tell you. I swerved across two lanes of traffic and back again whilst frantically trying to reach the lovely big bumble bee, before finally managing to pull off to the side of the road and remove my crash helmet. I have no idea how I missed all the other vehicles and how I didn't end up as just another piece of road pizza. Once I'd put my heart back in my chest I had time to consciously and logically think about how stupid my reaction had been - a bee sting although painful, is a lot less painful (or terminal) than hitting a 30 ton truck at 70 miles per hour. I never did find that lovely big bumble bee!

Just going back to motivation for a moment – was my reaction to having a lovely big bumble bee fly into my crash helmet negatively or positively motivated? Obviously it was negatively motivated – my outcome was to get the bee out of my crash helmet without being stung and I ended up at the mercy of the environment in which I found myself. Luckily for me the outcome was not negative but I cannot stress strongly enough that that was not under my control.

Once my unconscious mind had produced the picture of me not wanting to be stung by my lovely big bumble bee, a chain of events was put into play, a strategy made of thoughts, each of which produced a picture. This in turn triggered a biochemical cascade to be initiated that played out though my brain and body and inevitably produced a behavioural response. In the case of my lovely big bumble bee, it was to get the bee out of my crash helmet before it stung me, so I was negatively motivated to avoid being stung. From that moment on I was also most definitely at the mercy of my environment.

If you think of food, even if you're trying to avoid it, you'll start to feel hungry. In fact the more you think about it or the more you try not to think about food, the hungrier you'll usually become. What do you think of when you smell bacon frying? For most people the smell of frying bacon will instantly make them feel hungry. Even vegetarians will often say that the smell of bacon frying makes them hungry or even want to eat bacon. It doesn't matter what you might consciously think about eating meat, whether you abstain for moral, ethical or religious reasons or you simply don't like meat, when most people smell bacon cooking their unconscious mind will generate a picture and produce a response or behaviour – they feel hungry.

Have you ever tried not to stare at someone who has an unusual facial feature? You already know the more you tell yourself not to stare the more you can't help but stare.

"Mole, what mole? I can't see any mole".
Austin Powers.

It's your unconscious mind giving you the thing you're thinking of because it cannot process a negative. Instead of "don't stare at that person" all your unconscious sees is you staring at that person and thinks "OK I'll make you do that then".

A recent, hilarious, and now thanks to YouTube, a notorious, example of an unconscious mind being unable to not think of something and therefore producing a behaviour at odds with the conscious mind, happened on the BBC4's Today Programme. The brilliant and "usually" extremely professional presenter James Naughtie was telling the listeners there was to be an interview with the Culture secretary Jeremy "Hunt" (you may already be ahead of me here). Unfortunately for the brilliant and "usually" extremely professional Mr Naughtie, instead of saying Mr "Hunt" he said Mr "Cunt". As if that wasn't bad enough, to add insult to injury, to rub salt into Mr Hunt's already open wounds, on the very same day shortly after James Naughtie's little faux pas, Andrew Marr did exactly the same thing immediately after saying that they wouldn't make the same mistake. You just know they both had the "C" word in their heads and were both telling themselves not to say it at the exact moment they tried to say the word "Hunt".

This is the same reason a smoker might say "I really have to stop smoking before these things kill me" as they are in the very act of putting a cigarette to their mouth and lighting it – the unconscious thought which produces the action or behaviour does not match the conscious thought. In fact in this scenario the behaviour is completely at odds with the conscious thought. This is also the reason why anti-smoking advertising doesn't work despite the fact that all smokers (whether they want to smoke or not) are consciously aware of the dangers of smoking. In fact all smokers (and I can say this from years of experience as an ex-heavy smoker) already know how expensive, smelly and antisocial smoking is. And yet no matter how much their conscious mind or the negative advertising reminds them of these facts they continue to smoke, because no matter what conscious thought they have about smoking, all their unconscious mind sees is them smoking and it produces the behaviour to give it to them. Again I will go into more detail on getting the things we think about in the chapter on The Law of Attraction.

Summary

- Your unconscious mind codes your thoughts in pictures.
- Your unconscious mind cannot process a negative.
- You cannot NOT think of something

In the next chapter we will investigate the concept of existence only being possible because you exist and the impact this has on everything and everyone you know.

Chapter 14

What You See Is What You Get

Given everything you now know about how you create your own reality, how you take in such a tiny fraction of information about the real world and then delete, distort and generalise it beyond all recognition, before adjusting it depending on your state and physiology and then casting it out there to produce your map of the world, how real do you believe your world actually is?

I wonder, how important do you think you are to those who love you? To your friends? Enemies? Colleagues? Even to me?

I Think, Therefore You Are

Everything you know about the world, absolutely everything, everything that has ever existed, does exist and will exist in your world, only does so because you exist.

To fully understand that statement you must first fully understand that everything you know about the world doesn't come from out there but from inside your own head – remember, perception is projection. You, me and everyone else, we all take in such a small amount of information that it couldn't possibly create the lush, rich world we experience. Just as a film strip is made up of individual picture frames that look like a moving picture when run as a sequence because our minds fill in the blanks, the same thing happens in our own experience of the world. There is so much information available to us that if we were to physically process every bit of data we would need heads the size of St Paul's Cathedral just to accommodate our monstrous brains.

I wonder if you can imagine for a moment that you had never existed – not just that you had never been born because that implies you could have existed – but that you had never ever existed. What would or could exist given that your entire world, life, the universe and everything only ever existed because you were there to create and experience it in the first place?

A lot of people struggle with the idea of "nothing". It is such an abstract concept for the human mind to understand what nothing could possibly be. Have you ever wondered what being dead would be like? Most people think of being dead as similar to being asleep or being unconscious, which is why people worry about being buried or cremated and what sort of coffin to have, etc. Even the decision about whether or not to be an organ donor and if so which organs to donate is affected by not understanding that being dead means there is absolutely nothing, not even the absence of everything because to assume the absence of everything suggests there could be something; but simply nothing. Obviously I'm talking about a conscious awareness – your energy is still around because energy cannot be created or destroyed, only changed from one form to another.

But even the idea of death suggests the possibility of life. Having never been born, having never existed would mean there was nothing. Because we have no experience of "nothing" it can be incredibly difficult to understand what nothing really is. It's a similar problem when trying to get ones heads around the concept of geological time. We can imagine days, years and decades because as humans these are time frames we can experience. We can even think in terms of a hundred years or so. However as we start to think about longer time frames such as thousands of years or hundreds of thousands of years it becomes more and more difficult because it's not something we can experience. So when evolutionists, geologists and cosmologists and the like talk in terms of millions or hundreds of millions or even billions of years it becomes so abstract that it is almost impossible for the human mind to comprehend – even those who do probably don't!

Everything you experience in your world you only experience because you are here to both create and experience it; which is the same as everything only exists because you exist. In which case if you have children how could they exist if you never did? How could your parents exist if you never did? How could I have existed and written the very book that you are now reading if you had never existed? Everything you know and understand, everyone and everything in your world could and does only exist because you exist. As far as your world goes, life the universe and everything only began when you did.

Let's go back to Table 4 in Chapter 9 for a moment. In your relationship with the people on your VIP list, who do you think you were being the best you could be for, rather than the best you could be for you?

Now - because you are reading this book there is a good chance that you have something you would like to change or improve in your life – you are looking for some sort of personal development, in which case now is the time, the moment that you need to be putting on your own metaphorical oxygen mask. This is the time that you need to decide to put your name at the top of the list because when you have taken care of yourself, when you are living your life to the full, because you are the best you can be for you, you will also be the best for all those around you.

Whether it's being a passenger on a plane or bringing up kids, being at work or in any other aspect of your life, when you are the best that you can be for you, you will always be the best that you can be for everyone around you – especially for everyone on your list of VIPs.

Summary

- Everything in the universe only exists because you exist.

- You are "the" most important person in your world..

- By becoming the best that you can be for you, you become the best you can be for everyone else in your world.

In chapter fifteen we will look at cause and effect and at how your thinking patterns determine whether or not you are in control of your life. Are you just a victim of your life without any say in your own destiny? We also see how re-framing can give you back responsibility and ultimately control over your life.

Chapter 15

Cause And Effect

You've probably heard people refer to the term "cause and effect" on many occasions, but if you were to think of it as an equation, on which side of that equation do you think you might be on?

$$\text{cause} \longleftrightarrow \text{effect}$$

Whatever side they "think" they may be on, most people tend to be well and truly on the effect side of the equation. Unfortunately for most people, this is not a good place to be because it means that most people are under the effect of a cause that they believe is outside of their control – they are "at effect".

Before retraining as a hypnotherapist I worked for the NHS at a high secure forensic psychiatric hospital that accommodates some of the most disturbed, dangerous and interesting people in the United Kingdom. Like many people starting work in such a place, I believed my biggest worry would be meeting the patients and yet that's not what happened at all.

Everyone who works in a psychiatric hospital or any other such place that cares for vulnerable people has to undergo an enhanced Criminal Records Bureau (CRB) check. A CRB check will show whether or not you have any previous criminal convictions and it can take several weeks before the results come back. When the date arrived for me to begin working at the hospital the results of my CRB check had still not come back but it was important that I should start work as soon as possible. As I would not be working directly with the patients the only concern was that of security and so it was decided I could start my new job, but until my CRB check came back I would not be given access to any keys and passes etc. This was the case for about two weeks which meant that wherever I wanted to go in the hospital, even if it were only to the canteen, I would have to phone security and wait for someone to come and take me to where I needed to be. I would then be locked in and the process was repeated when I had finished and wanted to return to my office or visit another part of the hospital.

To my surprise I found this to be a very unnerving experience the cause of which at the time I could not understand – I knew I was safe, I didn't suffer from claustrophobia and I was never in any danger. So why on Earth did I feel so uncomfortable? Prior to starting work at the hospital, I thought I was going to be worried about the patients but it was the fact that I had no keys that really bothered me.

At the time I had no idea why I felt so vulnerable but looking back I can now see exactly why I felt that way. It was clearly and simply because I was not in control. As a consequence of the situation I was in I had no choice but to give total responsibility for my movements, my safety and my freedom, to other people. I was most definitely on the effect side of the equation; I was at effect. Due to the circumstances I had found myself in I had to give away all control over my freedom and movements while at work to "it, they, them, that - "it" being the CRB check, "they" being the Criminal Records Bureau, "them" being security and "that" being every door I did not have a key for.

"Well I've got news for you Dennis Doyle from downstairs, it's all your fault".
Mr. Ghoshdastidar.

To be at effect means you will play the part of the victim, the person to whom things happen. You have no choice and no say in your own life, you are a victim of fate, destiny, God, it, they, them, that.

Think of the people you know best; family, friends, colleagues and even yourself. How many of them would you say are on the effect side of the cause and effect equation? Who do you know who is at effect? Are they unhappy for some reason such as a partner who annoys them or doesn't treat them the way they feel they should be treated? Are they annoyed because their children aren't turning out the way they'd planned? Do they believe they are being held back in their career perhaps? Are they the sort of person who constantly whinges about the state of the country and the government and yet they never vote? I'm sure we all know at least one person for whom nothing ever goes right and whose life seems to be one drama after another but as far as they are concerned, it is never their fault. Have you ever tried to give such a person advice? "Why don't you...." to which they likely replied "I can't because.....". This is someone who is at effect. You may be able see the answer to their problem but they can't or won't, even when it's pointed out to them. They are under the effect of "it, they, them, that" and so they believe they have no power to change the situation. Perhaps there are times in your life when you are that person.

A classic example of being at effect can often be seen exhibited by some elderly people with regards to computers and technology.

"Oh no, I don't understand computers, its fine if you're young but I'm too old to learn about them now".
Some Elderly People.

Think about the times you have felt powerless or not in control – what or who was the cause of those situations?

When you are not in control or when you feel powerless it's because you have given control to "it, they, them, that" - you are "at effect". You are under the effect of an external cause.

Now think back to the times when you felt confident, when you were doing what you wanted to do – who or what was the cause then? The chances are it was you – in fact there was no chance, it was you! You were "at cause".

To be at "cause" means that you are responsible for everything that happens in your world. Yes, obviously "shit happens" to all of us from time to time but it's not what happens to us that's important but the choices we make in response to shit happening that's the crucial thing. It's the choices we make that determine whether or not we are responsible and therefore whether we are at cause or at effect.

"It's not whether you get knocked down; it's whether you get back up"
Vince Lombardi.

Being "at cause" is about being in control of "you" when things happen, because as we all know all too well, things happen whether we like it or not. However, by taking responsibility for the decisions you make, you put yourself back in control and ultimately onto the "cause" side of the equation – you are "at cause" and that's a nice place to be, ask any true Successful.

This is the reason people who witness, or just hear about something bad happening to someone else may say, "I wish it had happened to me instead of them". This is because most people are able to empathise with others and when they witness a negative event happening to someone else they have no control over the outcome, which puts them at effect, even though they are not involved or affected physically by that event. If on the other hand the event had happened to them, they would have been able to take responsibility for the event and therefore they would have been at cause.

Even when you have to do things that you may not want to do, if you have the mind-set that you have made the decision to do it then you are in control. For example, if you need to have a broken tooth removed because it's gone rotten and causing an infection, whether or not you like going to the dentist is not important because it is going to happen either way. If you really hate going to the dentist and have to be dragged along kicking and screaming then not only are you going to have a tooth removed but you are also going to suffer a great deal of stress and anxiety and even trauma. However, if you accept that you do not like going to the dentist but this is something that needs to be done for your own health, you will still have the tooth removed but without all the drama. Either way the tooth is coming out!

Summary

- To be 'at effect' means that you have given control to it, they, them, that.

- Being 'at effect' is not a comfortable place to be.

- To be 'at cause' means that you are responsible for your life – you are the cause of the things that happen in your life.

- By being 'at cause', you take responsibility for your life.

- All true Successfuls are 'at cause'.

- Most people are 'at effect'.

- To be one of the Successfuls you must be "at cause".

In the next chapter we look at the difference between positive thinking and on-par thinking and the difference each can make to your life.

Chapter 16

Positive Thinking vs on-PAR Thinking

You may have heard of the term "positive thinking" which was a lifestyle concept that became very big during the 60's and 70's and is still bandied about today for all sorts of things. The way I remember it being explained many years ago is that it worked on the premise that if you only think positively then nothing negative can happen to you – fill your life with positive things so there will be no room left for anything negative to get in. This is fine – up to a point. However, where positive thinking as a strategy falls down is that it doesn't take into account people and events outside of your control, which unfortunately happens to be just about everything and everybody.

Imagine for a moment that you are on your way to your favourite café to meet up with some of your best friends for a coffee and a good old gossip – you could of course also choose tea or even a hot chocolate with melted marshmallows in it should you wish, I'll leave the choice of beverage entirely up to you. You're feeling very positive, you just know that only good things can happen to you because you are only having positive thoughts, you only see the good in the world and everything is great in your life. You can't wait to hear how well your friends are doing because just like you, they are all positive thinkers too, and you're longing to tell them about just how well things are going for you right now – your business is booming, your social life has never been better, your relationship with your partner is amazing... and your sex-life – wow! You look across the street and see the coffee shop where you've arranged to meet up and there at the table in the window are your friends, all chatting and laughing as they wait for you to arrive. It's a stunningly beautiful spring day; the sun is shining down from a cloudless blues sky and the birds are singing in the trees that are just starting to burst in to life on this wonderful imaginary spring morning. You notice that your friends have spotted you and you start to wave at them as you begin to make your way across the road, all the while taking in the full beauty of the day and the all the wonder and majesty of life. In fact you're still waving to your friends as the bus runs straight over you killing you instantly!

Unfortunately for you, the day before this most tragic event, the driver of the bus found out that his wife had been having an affair and was leaving him for his best friend. He was so devastated by this news that he had gone out that evening and quaffed great quantities of alcohol, as though quaffing great quantities of alcohol was going out of fashion and he kept quaffing until unconsciousness wrapped him up in the big warm duvet of oblivion. By the time he'd woken up, ironically feeling as though he'd been run over by a bus, his wife had already moved out and on top of that he was now covered in his own vomit and he was late for work – the driver of the bus was not thinking at all positively.

You see, positive thinking as a concept can only work if everything in the universe is under your control and unless your name is God that is highly unlikely. With "positive thinking" you are putting the events that happen in your life outside of your control. You are effectively taking "your" responsibility for everything that happens to you and giving it to "it, they, them, that" and as we saw in Chapter 6 that is never going to end well.

On PAR thinking on the other hand allows one to take full control and responsibility for everything and anything that happens in one's life. Let's look again at the scenario of the coffee shop and the bus driver. In this example I asked you to imagine that you were a believer in positive thinking so that when you needed to cross the road to get to the coffee shop "you just knew nothing bad could happen". Can you see the problem with that statement? It's negatively motivated to avoid anything bad happening. Now I'd like you to imagine exactly the same scenario but this time as someone who understands and uses on-PAR thinking.

When you cross the road what is your goal? Is it to not get run over by a bus, or is it to get to the other side safely? By thinking about crossing the road safely you will have to make sure the road is safe for you to cross.

Yes, things that we are not expecting or that we would sooner didn't happen to us, do in fact happen to us from time to time, but it is our reaction to those events, it's the choices we make that determine whether or not our outcome is positive or negative.

Summary

- Positive thinking works on the belief that if you only have positive thoughts nothing bad can happen to you.

- Positive thinking removes your responsibility.

- Positive thinking moves you to the effect side of the equation.

- On-PAR thinking keeps you in control.

- On-PAR thinking gives you responsibility.

- On-PAR thinking moves you on to the cause side of the cause and effect equation – it allows you to be "at cause".

In the next chapter we will look at the law of attraction and how it can be used to attract the things you want into your world.

Chapter 17

The Law of Attraction

By understanding how your thoughts affect the world you experience, you are able to utilise the most powerful force in the universe – that is "The Law Of Attraction".

The law of attraction is as simple as it is powerful. In essence the concept runs along the lines that our thoughts determine what we attract into our lives. If we think about positive things, the things we "do" want (when we are positively motivated) we attract positive things; conversely, if we focus on negative things, the things we "don't" want (when we are negatively motivated) we attract negative things into our lives.

The law of attraction as I understand it differs from positive thinking in that when your goals are on PAR, it puts you in control of the events in your life. If you would be so kind as to cast your mind back to "Mark's Universal Law of Motivation" Part One, Chapter Five, you may recall that I suggest that motivation only stops when it meets an equal or greater force such as your outcome. The law of attraction however differs from motivation in that it never, ever, stops working. Like gravity it is constant and never-ending.

For me, the law of attraction works on two levels and in two very distinct ways. The first and most obvious is the ability of our unconscious mind to filter information coming to us from the outside world. Do you remember the NLP communication model in chapter eight? It explains so simply the way in which we filter information (data) coming to us from out there in the big wide world. This allows us to focus in on the things that we are thinking of, and as we already know, our unconscious mind will move mountains to give us the thing we are thinking about (whether it's the thing we want or the thing we don't want).

Have you ever noticed how groups of people who enjoy being together tend to be very similar people? Think of all the couples you know – if you were to rate their style or appearance would they be similar or worlds apart? Would one be suave and sophisticated while the other was a complete chav? There are always exceptions to any rule of course but in general most couples suit each other. The reason is that people who are like each other, like each other or "like people like people".

We are always on the lookout for people like ourselves, people we feel comfortable and safe with. We like to be around people of a similar intellectual level, people who have the same outlook on life and are interested in the same things as us. Our filtering system allows us to delete the information we are not interested in and focus on those people who do interest us.

Just like breathing, we are all constantly filtering information though we may not always notice it until it is pointed out – now you can notice your breathing because you are filtering out the unnecessary information to allow you to focus on it.

Have you ever had something specific on your mind such as thinking about a particular celebrity or a holiday destination you fancy going to or a type of food you'd like to try and all of a sudden you see it everywhere? The first time I noticed this effect, though at the time I didn't know how it happened, was several years ago when I was looking to buy a new car. I had taken a Saab 95 for a test drive. Until that day I hadn't really noticed Saab cars but no sooner was I was thinking of buying one I saw them everywhere. Not just Saab cars but silver Saab 95 Linears, just like the one I had taken for a test drive.

The following stories are excellent examples of the Law Of Attraction working through filtering. It also demonstrates the second way in which the Law Of Attraction works which I shall come to a little later.

Several years ago, a woman whom I shall call Debbie came to see me and during the course of our discussions she mentioned a problem she was having at work – it had nothing to do with why she had come to see me but had simply come up in conversation. Debbie told me she worked in retail and had been doing the same job for at least ten years and that she really loved it – or at least she used to. However, over the last several years she had noticed a change in the attitude of her customers. According to Debbie, for some reason she could not understand, every customer she had dealt with in the last five years or so seemed to be aggressive or rude. She thought they were always trying to get something for nothing and that this was now making her very disillusioned with her job.

I have to say that I found it a bit of a coincidence that after five years or so in the job "all" of her customers had suddenly changed from happy, enthusiastic buyers into grumpy, aggressive people trying to get something for nothing, so I asked her if she would be happy to take part in a little experiment. She had come to see me on a Friday afternoon and would not be back at work until Monday morning. I asked her if every time a customer entered the shop she would pretend that they were friends. I asked her to do her best to imagine how she would talk, move, act and behave if they really were her friends. I also wanted Debbie to imagine that every customer who came into her shop on Monday would genuinely want and need her help in choosing a product, and that on her part all she wanted to do was to help them make the right choice. She was to let me know what happened at our next meeting. Somewhere around lunchtime on the Monday however, I received an email from Debbie telling me that the experiment wasn't working because every customer who had come into the shop that morning had been like the customers she used to have – friendly, looking for advice and happy to be buying from her.

So what had happened to Debbie's customers? Was it just another coincidence that on the day of our experiment every one of her customers just happened to be friendly? I replied to Debbie's email asking how likely she thought it was that after five years of "bad" customers, on the very day of the experiment, only "good" customers visited the shop? So, was it the customers who had changed or something about Debbie that changed her belief in them?

Obviously the customers were still the same customers so it must have been something about Debbie that was different. Actually two things had changed about Debbie, the first of which we have just covered – the ability of her unconscious mind to filter information. By taking part in my little experiment Debbie was actively looking for "friendly, looking-for-advice and happy-to-be-buying-from-her" type customers, and so she was busy filtering the information in order to focus on what she was looking for.

This would also have been the case from the customer's point of view. By Debbie modelling her behaviour as if every customer was a friend, and by her acting as though that was genuinely the case – by walking, talking and behaving as though it were true, she would have been giving off all the physical signals of someone who wanted to help her customers and in return her customers would have felt relaxed around her and believe that she could be trusted to find them the right product at a good price.

So, simply by changing her belief about her customers, Debbie was able to radically change the reality of the situation. In the same way that my own belief that talking in front of people was a traumatic event had changed, so had Debbie's belief in her customers, simply by acting or "modelling" the behaviour she would exhibit with her real friends. Simply by modelling her behaviour on how she believed she would act if all her customers were "friendly, looking-for-advice and happy-to-be-buying-from-her" types,

Debbie was able to see for herself that she could change her reality.

When I lived in Cardiff (did I mention that I really like Cardiff?) and when we could afford it (and often even when we couldn't), myself and a group of my friends used to love going into town at night because there was always something happening, such a band or DJ we liked playing at Clwb Ifor Bach or at The Four Bars Inn, or one of the other excellent venues Cardiff had to offer at that time. Many bars and clubs also played certain genres of music that we were into in those days. Almost everyone within our group of friends seemed to have the same positive belief about Cardiff with the exception of one, who for the purpose of this anecdote shall be called Bob. Anyway our friend Bob for whatever reason had a completely different belief about the great city of Cardiff than the rest of us. Bob's belief was that it was a rough place, with constant fighting in the pubs and clubs, and so as a consequence we usually had to work hard to persuade him to come out with us. At that time we were all heavily into the music scene – in fact I was lucky enough to be in a band called "Rebecca's Daughters" with three of the friends from this social circle. We'd named that band after the Rebecca riots

184

in South Wales at the turn of the 19th century - oh we were such rebels.

I remember on one particular night a group of us went to a pub just off St Mary's Street to watch some other friends of ours play in their band. So there we were, a group of friends on a night out in a friendly pub that we knew well, watching some more of our friends play in their band in front of more friends and friends of friends – do you know I don't think it could have been a more friend-friendly event if it had taken place on the actual set of the American sitcom Friends. At the end of the night we'd all had a bloody good time, although I do remember I hadn't seen Bob in the pub for the last hour or so. I did however meet up with Bob a few days later and was shocked to see him sporting a rather impressive black eye! He explained that he had somehow gotten into a scuffle on his way to the toilet which had resulted in him being thrown out of the pub. At the time I wondered how on Earth it was possible that we could go out as a group of friends to the friendliest friend-friendly venue in Cardiff and all have a great time except Bob who managed to get thrown out along with his shiny new black eye?

Now Bob himself is not a violent person; far from it. He is a kind, gentle pacifist type – we all were; so why amongst all of us did he find trouble when everyone else found a good time? As I said, at the time I had no idea how this could happen but now I have some understanding of the concepts of NLP, I can see it was because "trouble" was exactly what his unconscious mind was looking for. You see, when the rest of us were thinking of a night out we were looking for a fun time, for a great evening, for interesting people to meet and talk drunken nonsense with and for some great music to sing and dance to. Those were the pictures our unconscious minds could see and our unconscious minds did everything they could to give it to us by filtering out any information that didn't fit in with our goal. However, when Bob was thinking about the same night out, his thoughts were of "not" having a bad time, of "not" getting into a fight, of "not" meeting violent drunks and "not" getting thrown out of the pub. If you cast your mind back to Chapter Thirteen where we learnt that the unconscious mind cannot process a negative – remember the "don't think of a tree" exercise - what sort of pictures do you think Bob's unconscious mind was seeing? Exactly - if you take the negative word "not" from the things Bob was thinking of then his unconscious mind was in fact seeing pictures that related to "having" a bad time, of "getting" in to a fight, of "meeting" violent drunks and "getting" thrown out of the pub and that is exactly what his unconscious mind gave him. Bob's unconscious mind filtered out all the unnecessary information, which allowed him to focus on and find the one person during the whole of that evening who would be kind enough to give him his shiny new black eye.

In the story earlier about Debbie and her customers, Debbie had gotten into a thinking strategy of "not" wanting bad customers (and therefore ironically looking for them) and that's exactly what she found, every working day for more than five years. Her unconscious mind was seeing the pictures of bad customers and was happily filtering out (or deleting, distorting and generalising) anything that was not needed in order for her to find bad customers. When she started to look for good customers that was what she found, because just like you, me and the rest of mankind, Debbie's unconscious mind filtered out the data she did not need (deletion, distortion and generalisation) and focused on the data she did need according to her thinking strategy. This also caused Debbie to change her behaviour and become the person her customers wanted to deal with – remember "like people, like people". Exactly the same thing was happening to Bob. His focus was "not" to find people who might want to fight him and so ironically he spent all evening looking for them and without fail every time he was out for a night in Cardiff they would find him.

The astute may have noticed that I said "they would find him" even though I was describing him looking for them in order that he could avoid them. The reason for this apparent dichotomy can be explained by the second way in which the Law Of Attraction works.

With the exception of a few odd anomalies such as Neutrinos, everything in the universe, from a single atom, to a tiny grain of sand, to a hypnotherapist, to a Blue Whale, to the largest planets and stars in the cosmos has both mass and energy. It was once thought that mass and energy were two separate things; that was of course until Albert Einstein developed his special theory of relativity. The relationship between the mass and the energy of something is described in what is probably now the most famous equation in the world of science,

$$E = mc^2$$

What this equation tells us is that all things that have mass also have energy and the two are observed as an entity called the mass-energy equivalence.

The important thing for us with regards to the Law Of Attraction is that energy is broadcast as a wave with specific frequencies depending on the mass in question. For example, when sodium atoms are excited by an electric current they throw off photons that travel in a wave of a particular length and frequency that we see as yellow light. That is why most UK street lights appear yellow – because they are high-pressure sodium lamps. Scientists can even tell what gasses are present in the atmosphere of planets many light years away just by looking at the spectrum of light they give off.

A similar thing happens with sound; if I pluck the E string on my guitar it sends out a wave of energy that I hear as the tone I know as E or as my parents know as a loud noise. The interesting thing is that if I pluck an E sting on one guitar it has the effect of causing the E strings on other guitars nearby to resonate too. A well-known physics experiment uses tuning forks to reproduce this effect. A wooden sounding board is loaded with tuning forks tuned to various frequencies. When a tuning fork of a particular frequency is activated and placed on the same sounding board as the other tuning forks, it causes all the tuning forks tuned to the same pitch to resonate. Tuning forks tuned to different pitches will remain silent however.

Research has shown that thoughts are energy and that every thought we have produces a wave with its own resonance which is cast out into the universe just like the sound produced by a guitar string or the light from distant stars. Every second of every day we are all transmitting energy signals produced from the thoughts we have. Not only are we transmitting signals in the form of energy waves but we are also receiving energy from other people, animals and objects – remember everything that has a mass has energy and is therefore transmitting energy.

If you cast your mind back again to the NLP Communication Model, I described how we filter information coming in to us from the outside world. However, this is only part of the information we analyse. Just like tuning forks we also resonate to certain frequencies, so when we meet a new group of people we will be drawn towards the people who give off a frequency that excites us – the people we are in tune with.

Conversely we are repelled by those with whom we are completely out of phase.

This attraction is not only limited to other people but to the very things you think about. Like attracts like. Things that resonate at the same frequency are in harmony and tend to attract each other.

Have you ever noticed how things seem to go from bad to worse when you are having a bad day? On the other hand, when you are "on a roll" things just seem to go your way and fall in to place. This is the Law Of Attraction at work. You are literally creating the world around you as you think – or rather you are attracting the world around you with your thoughts.

The Law Of Attraction is a universal force of nature that anyone can use to create the life they desire. If you want a particular lifestyle or a particular job, social group, house or whatever; if you want to be a Successful, then by focusing on having those things, by being that person, by being a Successful, you will begin to attract them into your life.

I would say that the Law of Attraction is one of the most powerful tools I use, both with my clients and in my own life. It has probably been one of the strongest drivers when I look back at the changes I've made in my life.

Summary

- The Law Of Attraction is the most powerful force in the universe.

- The Law Of Attraction never stops.

- You attract into your life the things you think about.

In the next chapter we will look at who is in control of your life:- is it you? Or is it "it, they, them, that"?

Chapter 18

Who's Driving The Bus

I'm sure you will have heard life being described as a journey and to me it really is like that because we all have a starting point and an end point. Along the way we visit many places and pick up and drop off various aspects of our lives such as our beliefs, learnings, likes, dislikes and fears, people, relationships and vocations and vacations, have success and failures and experiences of all kinds. The question is who is it that is deciding what you are experiencing? In other words, if life is a journey who's driving the bus? Is it you or is it "it, they, them, that"? Has the answer changed since you started reading this book – since you began this particular part of your journey? If so, in what way? If not, what other resources do you need to put into action to take control of your journey, to become the driver of your bus?

Exercise 4.

In a moment I'd like you to close your eyes and imagine you are a passenger on a bus. As you sit in your seat and gaze out of the window I want you to notice the world passing you by – or more accurately, I want you to notice "your" world passing by the window. Take a few minutes doing this so that you can allow your mind to bring up any aspects of your life it chooses and you can take your time to observe them as your bus moves along through your life. After a few minutes or when you feel ready, you can open your eyes again and take a moment to think about what you have seen. I want you to ask yourself this question: "is the world I have just travelled through the world I want"? When you look out of the bus do you see a life of your choosing passing the windows or a life that you have been given - a life that is not of your making?

At some point in all of our lives we will inevitably reach the end point and when your time comes and you're lying there in your bed at the end of your life – hopefully in many, many years' time, you will have the opportunity to look back on your life. At that moment you will either say "yeah I did all that" or "doh! I didn't want to do any of that". So, read through the above paragraph again so that you know what you need to do and then, when you're ready, make yourself nice and comfortable, take a deep breath and allow your eyes to close. Once you're sitting or lying comfortably with your eyes closed begin to imagine being a passenger looking out of the window of a bus. You can see your life passing by outside and as you travel through it you notice different parts of your life - you allow yourself to see different things that you have done or things you didn't do and I want you to note whether or not they were your choices or the choices of "it, they, them, that"? Please do that now before moving on!

So, was the life you saw passing the windows of your bus the life that you want to live? Or, was the life that you watched pass by the window a life that you feel is not under your control? If you witnessed a life that was not of your choosing then now is the time to take action because the only point of power in your life is right now. You didn't do anything to change the situation yesterday and because tomorrow never gets here you won't be doing anything to change your life then either, so now is the most powerful time you have.

If you could have the life you want, if you could do the things you want to do and be the person you want to be, what would that life look like? Imagine what you would be able to see from the window of your bus if the images that passed by were all from aspects of your life that you chose to do? Imagine what success would look like, and has it changed from the time you started this book? If life is a journey but it isn't going in the direction you wish to go, then you need to ask yourself the question "who's driving the bus"? If you aren't going in the direction you want to be going then sure as eggs it is not going to be you in the driver's seat and the only way you are going to be able to change direction is for you to become the driver.

Exercise 5.

In a moment I want you to close your eyes again and find yourself back on your bus as it travels through your life. Just as before I want you to look out of the window and notice your life as it moves along, notice all the things that have happened in your that life, all the things that you did not choose and that you believe were out of your control. As you watch these parts of your live drift past the window I want you to ask yourself another question. If this is supposed to be your life then who is driving the bus? As you think of this I want you to imagine that you are getting up and walking to the front of the bus. As you reach the front of the bus I want you to look and see who or what is actually driving the bus. Now is the time to make a choice. Now is the time for you to take control. Picture yourself pulling the who or what out of the driver's seat and throwing it off the bus. Now you sit in the driver's seat. Feel the seat as you sit down, see your hands as they take hold of the steering wheel. Now look out of the huge front window at the life ahead of you – a life that you choose because you are now the driver of your bus.

This is an exercise that you can do whenever you feel that you are not going in the direction you want to be going in. It's an exercise you could use every morning before you even get out of bed if you wish. It only needs to take a minute or two for you to picture yourself in the driver's seat of your bus - think of how you want your day to go and visualise it in front of you as you drive towards it. By seeing yourself sitting in the driver's seat and by driving your bus in the direction you want to go, you will also be driving your bus from the effect side to the cause side of the cause and effect equation.

Summary

- The only point of power in your life is right now.
- In order for you to control of the direction of your life's journey, you have to be the driver of the bus.
- Whatever direction you choose for your life it must always be on PAR.

In the next chapter I will describe how we all already possess all the resources we need to become successful.

Chapter 19

You Already Have All The Resources

There are certain assumptions made in NLP known as "Presuppositions". These are things that NLP takes as read, or assumes to be true and one such presupposition is that we already possess within us all the resources needed to succeed. However, there are as many different interpretations of this assumption as there are NLP practitioners.

My first introduction to this particular presupposition was to be told that "we already possess all the resources we need to achieve anything we want in life" - something I never really gelled with as a concept for the obvious reason that there will always be some limiting factor or factors in certain situations.

If we think back to the example of Buster Martin, he most definitely possessed all the resources he needed to enter and take part in the London Marathon which was of course his goal (and his outcome). However, for obvious reasons he did not, nor would he ever possess the resources needed in order to win the London Marathon. For sure Buster may have possessed the necessary resources at some point in his earlier life but as the oldest man running the Marathon he could not have possessed the resources needed to win at the age of 101 or even at 94.

Again to help keep the book light, I don't want to go into presuppositions just now- perhaps that too will be in a future book along with strategies – who knows? For now I simply want to give you my take on this particular presupposition to which I have added a cheeky little caveat which in my world makes a lot more sense.

In my world I like to think of this particular presupposition in this way,

"We all possess within us all the resources needed to achieve any goal in life, so long as that goal is on PAR".

By adding the tag-line "so long as that goal is on PAR" it takes away the idea of chance and gives back responsibility to the subject – in this case, you!

Although we may not always be aware of it, every one of us regardless of age, sex, fitness level, education or starting position, already possesses all the resources within us to achieve anything we want in life "so long as our goal is on PAR".

How many times have we heard amazing stories of people turning their lives around by doing something even they never thought they were capable of, such as taking up long distance running or cycling in their late 30's – 40's and older. Often people who retire will take up sports, hobbies or even start a new business using skills and abilities they never even realised they possessed.

On the 5th May 1954 everyone knew that it was physically impossible for a human being to run a mile in under four minutes. Surely that was obvious to anyone with more than two brain cells - after all, hadn't people been competing in running races for thousands of years? Since the invention of the stopwatch not a single runner had broken the four minute mile barrier. So, as the world awoke on the morning of the 6th of May 1954 everyone still knew that it was not physically possible for a human being to run a mile in under four minutes – that was of course everyone except a 25 year old medical student from Harrow in Middlesex by the name of Roger Bannister.

Sir Roger Bannister, as he is now rightly known, was competing for the British Amateur Association at an event in Oxford, and prior to the meeting he had arranged for his two friends, Chris Brasher and Chris Chataway to act as pace-setters for the early part of the race. With their assistance he completed the first ¾ of a mile in less than three minutes and the final ¼ mile in under a minute finishing in a record (and myth) breaking time of 3:59:40 before collapsing exhausted in front of a rapturous crowd of spectators.

There are two things about this phenomenal story that jump straight out at me and they are: firstly that Roger Bannister knew that it was possible to break the four minute mile barrier despite all the so-called evidence to the contrary. As such, because he knew it was possible to run a mile in under four minutes, Roger Banister would have also known that he did in fact already have all the resources needed to break the four minute barrier. Secondly and much more telling than Roger Banister's amazing achievement is the fact that no sooner had this barrier been removed than Roger Banister's record was soon broken and then that record was broken and so on and so forth.

All of the world's top one mile runners already had the resources to run a mile in under four minutes but it was their beliefs that stopped them from accessing those resources needed to achieve it. It was Roger Bannister's belief about his ability to achieve his goal that allowed him to put in the necessary training, to develop the necessary skills and gain the power and stamina required to run a mile in under four minutes. Conversely, had he believed he could not run a mile in under four minutes then it's very likely that when the world went to sleep on the 6th May 1954 everyone would have still known that a human being could not run a mile in under 4 minutes.

When he stood on that starting line Roger Bannister knew he could do it – he knew he already possessed all the resources needed to break the four minute mile barrier.

Was Sir Roger Bannister's goal of running the mile in under four minutes on PAR? Was his goal positive? Yes, of course it is a positive thing to strive to be the best at something. Was his goal physically achievable? Yes, even though it had not been done before, Roger Bannister knew he had the physical ability to run the mile in under four minutes. Was his goal realistic? Yes, he was willing and able to put in the time and effort to develop the necessary skills to reach his goal. Was his outcome positive? Oh Yeah!!

Summary

You already possess all the resources needed to achieve anything you chose to do as long as your goal in on PAR

Chapter 20

The Finale

I became a therapist and personal development coach because of the amazing changes that have occurred in my own life. The knowledge and skills that I have gained over the years have continued to change and add to the dynamic richness of my life and I hope that by sharing my experiences, thoughts and ideas, you and everyone else who feels stuck with what you have, yet know you really do have something more to offer, can use the techniques and ideas in this book to move from being a follower, or being "at effect" to being a Successful, or "at cause". In the end, when all is said and done this is your life, you are only going to live it once – you really don't get to come back and have another go at it!

It is my sincere belief that if you put into practice the ideas and concepts and thinking patterns described in this book then in many, many years' time, when you are lying on your bed at the end of your days, you will be able to look back at your life and rather than thinking Doh, I didn't want to do any of that!! You will look back at all the things you have done - all the amazing things you have achieved and think YEAH - "I" did all of that!!!

The Successfuls aren't the people who are marketed to us on the TV and in glossy gossip magazines – no, those people are just the people who are marketed to us on the TV and in glossy gossip magazines. These people have photo-shopped lives but in reality they are no happier, no less depressed, no less anxious and no more relaxed than anyone else. They have exactly the same issues as the rest of us, if not more.

I, like most people in the Western world have spent much of my life being seduced by the promise that that car, those people, that drink, this lifestyle, these clothes, that drug or this personality would make me happy, but here's the thing – I never stopped to ask myself whether or not I was already happy. Did I already have the things I was looking for and if not why not? Was I being fed a false belief about what a Successful actually is by the media, society and my peers?

And the victims of their world,
Are advertised on posters,
Just a beach and a pretty girl,
You just take this potion.

The Levellers

Early on in my career as a therapist I worked with a client who started the whole "Successfuls" thing rattling around in my head. Margaret was, as far as anyone else knew, the epitome of a Successful; she had a wonderful social life, she was a very attractive, very intelligent, soft-spoken lady with a loving husband who was exceptionally gifted when it came to business which meant she had a lovely home life, nice cars, clothes, holidays etc. Also being a very wealthy woman in her own right Margaret had no money worries at all.

On her first visit to my office she arrived in a high-end 4x4 which I commented on as it's one of my all-time favourite cars. On her second visit she was driving another high-end car, this time a two seater convertible sports car and when I asked if she had changed cars she told me that this was her run-around. On her third and final visit she once again arrived in what looked like the same 4x4 she had driven on her first visit but was in fact as Margaret explained the brand new model that she recently bought because it had the latest engine.

As you can see Margaret would appear to be the stereotypical Successful, so it might surprise you to hear that Margaret came to see me because she was suffering from chronic anxiety, low self-confidence and low self-esteem. She had been on antidepressants for some time but like many, she had come to the conclusion that pills were not the answer.

In Chapter one I eluded to people getting their dreams, such as a young girl being spotted by a talent scout or the lucky lottery winners scooping the roll-over jackpot. "But Mark" I hear you cry "surely these are dreams that actually came true"? Well yes, I would have to agree that it would appear to be the case. From a distance and in your map of the world it may well look as though they have become part of the exclusive Successfuls club. However, is that really the case? What was it that they believed their dreams would give them? What was it that they wanted but didn't already have, that they believed their dream would allow them to get?

Let's look at the example of the young girl wanting to be a supermodel. What could it be that she (or possibly her mother) so badly wanted that only becoming a supermodel would provide? Fame? Wealth? Lifestyle? Adoration? But these are all concepts. None of them are real. You can't put any of them in a wheelbarrow – OK you can put money in a wheelbarrow, but not "wealth". As I said all the way back in Chapter 5 "Money in and of itself cannot "do" anything "to" us". It's a well-know fact that many supermodels suffer from eating disorders and there is a high rate of mental illness within the industry.

As for the lucky lottery winners, there are many stories about families being torn apart, marriages failing and winners losing all their money and filing for bankruptcy after winning the lottery.

Believing that you will only be happy when you get your dream is to give all responsibility for your own happiness to something you cannot put in to a wheel barrow. If you are trying to achieve a dream you will put all of your energy into something that will either never happen or is not under your control. This will inevitably lead to you becoming disheartened and give up and you will eventually believe that you have failed.

The biggest discovery for me is that the "Successfuls" don't actually have any special powers or super-human abilities. In fact the "Successfuls" don't even exist except in the minds of the people who observe them – those who believe the marketing hype. Remember perception is projection. If you are an angry person, if you are always annoyed and unhappy what difference would winning the lottery make to you? Would you lose your anger? Would you suddenly become a tolerant happy-go-lucky person? I can tell you from my experience of working with clients who already have everything we are told we need to have for us to be happy, if you are angry, annoyed and unhappy and you are lucky enough to win the lottery the only thing to change will be your bank balance.

As with everything else you create in your world, you also create the Successfuls but in reality they are just like anyone else. So who are the real Successfuls? Well, they are in fact very difficult to point out because you don't generally see them. Actually that's not strictly true, you do see them, you probably see them every day, you just don't know them as Successfuls.

Successfuls range from a school dinner lady to a Harley Street surgeon to a teacher to a homeless person to rock stars and film stars to a hermit living in a cave. The reason you do not know they are a Successful is because they do not feel the need to broadcast their success to the world.

What was your goal for reading this book? Has your goal changed or have you re-framed your original goal to bring it on PAR?

So what was my goal for writing this book?

- To pass on my experiences.
- To become an author.
- To make money.

In that order.

What is a Successful? I think that I now understand that being a Successful means that one is happy with one's life and has no need to justify one's own success. That doesn't mean that a Successful doesn't have things they want to achieve and goals they want to reach. The difference between a non-Successful and a Successful is that a Successful will answer the question "what do you want?" with the words "I want...."

As I said earlier "it is my belief that if you put into practice the ideas and concepts and thinking patterns described in this book you will be able to achieve any goal you set your mind to". You will be able to look back at your life, at all the things you have done - all the amazing things you have achieved and think "YEAH - I did all that" and this is the thing – it doesn't matter how much knowledge you have or how much natural talent you were born with, all the learnings and all the skill in the world mean absolutely nothing until you act. It's you that has to make the decision to put all your knowledge and skill into practice, to sit in the driver's seat of your bus and choose the direction of your own journey through life.

Obviously this book is not a text book or a definitive manual on how to live your life – there is no such book. These are merely my thoughts and beliefs based on my experiences both as a therapist and as a client. Hopefully this book will help you to change your life by discovering what success really means to you and help you find the resources you need to become one of the real Successfuls. If for you that means becoming a film star, or an astronaut, a teacher, a successful entrepreneur, a loving husband or wife or a sandwich packer, as long as your goal is on PAR you already have all the resources needed to achieve it. At the very least I hope that my musings will have introduced to you the concept of change and personal development and set you on the road as the driver of your own bus on your own journey through life.

So what was the obstacle stopping me from becoming a Successful? Me of course! Have I become one of the Successfuls? I have plenty of friends, I've met some wonderful people and I've done many amazing things in my life and intend to do a whole load more before leaving this mortal coil. I already was; I was just looking at my life through the wrong frame.

Remember To Remember

How many times have you forgotten something really important having told yourself "I mustn't forget.....", or forgotten to do something after being told by someone else "don't forget to....". Remember that the unconscious mind cannot processes a negative. So, after deleting the negative words "mustn't" and "don't" from those statements the unconscious mind only hears "I must forget......" and "do forget to" and it gives you exactly what you ask for. Like any other goal you want to achieve, remembering is not the same as not forgetting.

Remembering to set your alarm before going to bed, remembering to pick up the kids from school, remembering to say thank you, and remembering to remember the concepts and ideas in this book that will change your life, are all positives. They are all things that your unconscious mind can see and do it's best to give you.

Summary

Remember:

When you set yourself a goal, whether it's to find another job, a loving long-term relationship, improving your health, or anything to do with personal development; in fact any change you want to make in your life, or for any goal you want to reach, you must first answer the question "what is it that you want that you don't have now" exactly as it was asked.

Remember:

If you are positively motivated you will want to move towards your goal as opposed to being negatively motivated which means you are trying to move away from or avoid something.

Remember:

If you find that you are trying to get away from something, then you need to re-frame your goal so that you become positively motivated to move towards it.

Remember:

Your goal must be on PAR. There's no point in putting time and effort into reaching a goal, that isn't under your control. If your goal is positive, achievable and realistic then you already have all the resources needed to achieve it.

Remember:

If you are not living the life you want then you are at "effect". This means that you have given responsibility and control to "it, they, them, that". If things are not going your way then who is driving the bus?

Remember:

In order for you to be the best you can be for those around you, you must first be the best you can be for you. Without you there is literally nothing, so you are the most important person in your world.

Remember:

The Law of Attraction means that you attract into your life that which you focus on.

I shall finish up by quoting some amazing lyrics by the anarcho–punk band Crass.

Be exactly who you want to be, do what you want to do,
I am he and she is she but you're the only you,
No one else has got your eyes, can see the things you see,
It's up to you to change your life and my life's up to me.

Thank You

Printed in Great Britain
by Amazon.co.uk, Ltd.,
Marston Gate.